PARADOXES OF POWER

A Collection of Essays on Failed Leadership - and How to Fix It -

Edited by Carl W. Hunt
& Joshua M. Hunt

Local Buzz Business Solutions, LLC, Centennial, CO

ISBN: 9798685995278

Cover design by: Joshua M. Hunt
Cover Photo Credits: Left to Right: Mike Von, Library of Congress, Charles Deluvio, Don Fontijn, Markus Spiske, Ryan Kosmides...Thanks to Unsplashed.com.
Library of Congress Control Number: 2018675309
Printed in the United States of America

Dedicated To America's Young People

- The Future and Hope of our Nation -

Contents

Paradoxes of Power

A Collection of Essays on Failed Leadership

- and How to Fix It -

Edited by Carl W. Hunt and Joshua M. Hunt

With Walter E. Natemeyer, Lawrence A. Kuznar, Dennis W. Greene, C. E. Hunt, Marc Hill and Veronica A. Mata

With a Foreword by Stuart A. Kauffman, M.D., MacArthur Fellow

"Power concedes nothing without a demand. It never did and it never will."

\- Frederick Douglas, 1857, in his West
India Emancipation Speech
Canandaigua, NY

"When you see something that is not right, not just, not fair, you have a moral obligation to say something. To do something. Our children and their children will ask us, 'What did you do? What did you say?' For some, this vote may be hard. But we have a mission and a mandate to be on the right side of history."

\- Congressman John R. Lewis, December 2019 remarks
in the US House of Representatives on the impeachment
vote of President Donald Trump

Preface

Apart from Appendix A, the essays included in this book were written by folks whom few would know to be "Experts in their Fields." This is because these writers have been among the many quiet heroes of America who go about doing their jobs every day, taking care of their families, followers, patients or clients and learning the lessons of leadership from the ground-up.

There is one exception, however. Appendix A, as a detailed reference, sets up both theoretical and practical considerations of power and leadership, and applies them across a wide range of contexts. It establishes the baseline for the study of **Paradoxes of Power**, and as such, requires great expertise and experience from its author, Dr. Walter E. Natemeyer, an internationally known expert in explaining and teaching the concept of power. Walt is especially well versed in the aspects of social relationships that encompass power in various organizational settings. Please read it. It is also previewed in Chapter 0.5.

The additional authors have written their chapters to share first-hand knowledge and expertise, learned practically as well as studied in depth, and accumulated over years of successful relationships in their respective organizations. They consider themselves passionate seekers of *common-sense power relationships.* These relationships seek to benefit everyone involved and allow organizations to succeed as a whole and not just as imbalanced and disconnected parts.

Our collected essays will touch on all of this, as well as cover the changes that our society is experiencing through the COVID-19 Pandemic. Power relationships are changing, and common sense and humility must prevail as the global population learns to navigate a post-pandemic world as a team rather than a league of competitors. We focus on the improvement of race-, gender-, and governmental-power imbalances in relationships. Together, these concepts form the core of the proposals this book offers.

We published this book to help our youngest generations in America to better understand and appreciate the role that power plays in our societal relationships at every level. We do not seek to address every issue related to the failings of leadership power, but rather to introduce the issues to new generations of Americans who will soon take on the mantles of authority. We hope to help them frame their own questions about our country's past and future to better guide our continued development as a nation. These new questions are critical to outlining our future.

If **Paradoxes of Power** has a single mission, it is to help educate and encourage the future influencers, the future wielders and yielders of power, who will grow and shape the fate of humanity for years to come. The ability to recognize, avoid, and mitigate paradoxes in power relationships will be a critical tool in all of this, and our sincere hope is that this book can aid in that effort.

- Carl and Joshua, the Editors

Foreword

I have known Carl and Josh Hunt since 1997. Carl had just started the doctoral program at George Mason University in Virginia and his son Josh was only six when we met. Wife and mom Barbara Hunt cooked my team, Bios Group, a wonderful dinner that night in Springfield, Virginia and I knew we'd all be friends for a very long time. I am so delighted that they've teamed up to coauthor and serve as the principle editors of this book, Paradoxes of Power, and I feel compelled to tell their readers a little about how important this distinctive collection of essays is.

Within these pages, all generations of Americans will find insights on recognizing and mitigating paradox in what Carl and Josh call "power relationships" that most people may not have even realized existed. Paradox is a pernicious beast because it tricks us all into thinking everything is going along fine right up to the point that leaders, followers, and their organizations fall apart. This can be a catastrophe when that organization is an entire nation and that nation is the United States of America.

For at least the last 50 years, the United States has slowly drifted deeper into paradoxes of power in every type of organization and every area of leadership. This probably happens in all organizations from time-to-time, but when it happens to the nation that can credibly claim to be the greatest and freest on the planet, people everywhere are in trouble. The elections of 2016 highlighted just how much trouble we are all in and that's why this book is so important and timely.

I've been a scientist for 60 years, serving my community and our nation in a variety of capacities and have grown to appreciate the importance of good leadership in every organization of which I've been a part. Carl was one of the first to introduce me to the ideas about paradox in leadership as a discipline which could be identified and studied. As a scientist, I learned that studying a paradox of power could inform both leaders and followers about how it fosters the abuse and misuse of power. Thankfully, through this book, I've also learned how paradoxes can be mitigated through common sense approaches to leadership and followership, lessons I think Carl and Josh and their marvelous team of essayists have revealed.

Carl and Josh direct the lessons and challenges of *Paradoxes of Power* to our younger generations of Americans. It is they who take the reins of power in the coming years. The book's presentation of such a diverse representation of our nation, backed up by critical questions, frame the discussions we all need to have. This is essential to resolve our dilemmas of power in America from now on.

Paradoxes of Power is the right book for the right time in America. Read these essays, understand the lessons, absorb the questions we need to ask, and help make the United States of America **united** once again.

- Dr. Stuart A. Kauffman, MD, MacArthur Fellow, Fellow of the Royal Society of Canada

Santa Fe, New Mexico, September 1, 2020

Introduction

by Carl W. Hunt and Joshua M. Hunt, Editors

The American leadership power system is fractured. We've lost touch with how power relationships are supposed to work. We rarely acknowledge that these relationships should benefit both *wielders of* and *yielders to* their influence. As a result, our institutions, our nation, and almost every form of democratic republic may be worse off now than they have been in decades.

To be clear, power is not inherently bad. In fact, power relationships allow for success, and help to maintain societies and organizations of all sizes. Without power and influence, we as humans would find it nearly impossible to build anything beyond only the simplest of groups or teams. Leaders must emerge, and those leaders must make use of their followers' talents and resources to enable the growth and survival of their collective groups. Government, religion, family, business, those are just a few examples of ideas that would never have come to fruition were it not for power to motivate and organize towards a common goal.

But...how we use power has become a problem in our modern world, and we need to fix it. The survival of the species, as well as the survival of the planet, depends on choices we all make together, and we need those with power to start pushing us in the right direction.

This book is about transforming human relationships that are built around power. Over the last couple of decades, nations around the globe have seen shifts in how leaders lead and how followers follow. The flow of influence has changed, which has resulted in egregious misuses and misapplications of government over the governed. In the United States alone, we have seen failures at the Federal, state, and local levels. We have also observed failure at the social level by 'civilized' members of society who would still attempt to deny power and privilege based on gender, race, or sex. With the advent of social media and massive internet connectivity, these abuses of power have spilled over into all kinds of social relationships everywhere, and the consequences are echoing into nearly every aspect of our lives.

These failures of power relationships have dramatically reduced the effectiveness of government and have warped our perception of what a good leader should even look like. Our confidence has been shaken, and the notion of 'self-rule' finds new challenges from every direction. This is happening worldwide, but it is particularly visible in the United States, where we've strayed from the path that once led us towards a healthy future.

The editors, authors, and contributors to this book are all Americans, but we are also members of the global society, and we are concerned that the way power is being used today is creating paradoxes all around us. To illustrate, it's paradoxical that achieving balance between leaders and followers has even become a paradox. It should not be this complicated!

To start overcoming these paradoxes, we must understand where and how they originate. We'll talk about power relationships at every level: from government to governed, owners to employees and leaders to followers, to name a few. More importantly, we will suggest solutions, and attempt to demonstrate how success can emerge from failure when the right concepts and models are better understood.

Perspective, combined with the willingness to observe, analyze, and critique our domains of power are necessary to recognize their respective paradoxes. This process is vital to getting back on track as a country, and to making power work better for everyone in our post-pandemic world. Our belief is that a fresh examination holds the promise to make the United States of America *united* once again. The rest of the world will benefit as well. In the meantime, we invite you to please consider *Paradoxes of Power*.

0.5. The Substance Of Power: A Preview

by Walter E. Natemeyer

In 2001, Paul H. Hersey and I published a groundbreaking essay entitled "Situational Leadership and Power," in which we proposed that given the "integral relationship between leadership and power, leaders must not only assess their leader behavior in order to understand how they actually influence other people, but they must also examine their possession and use of power."[1] Hersey's and Kenneth Blanchard's model of Situational Leadership calls for leaders to adapt their leadership styles (direction and support) according to the followers' capacity for performance. It was one of the first models that demonstrated the importance of focusing on the followers' ability, willingness and confidence, known also as Readiness Level, when selecting leadership styles.

Hersey and I showed definitively that the application of power in an adaptive fashion was just as important as the situational approach to leadership styles. Leaders must have some sort of power to enable them to gain compliance and/or commitment from others. Of course, a corollary bottom line is that the followers must respond to that power for the compliance or commitment to be consummated. Matching followership readiness and power bases will greatly facilitate the style of leadership technique most likely to be effective in given situations.

Simply put, if leaders apply relevant and appropriate sources of power to a leader-follower relationship, they can avoid misfires in leadership, or what the editors and essayists of our new book assert is a **Paradox of Power**. There's more to the power relationship than leadership style, readiness of followers and bases of power, but these are critically important components of the power relationship needed to avoid paradoxes. If leaders apply power correctly, they are more likely to use the appropriate leadership style as well.

Leadership is an attempt to influence another individual or group; it is an influence process. A good way to think about this is that Power *is influence potential*—the resource that enables a leader to gain compliance or commitment from others. Despite its critical importance, power is a subject that is often avoided, for power can have an unpleasant side; many people may want to wish it away and pretend it is not there, but power is a real-world issue. Leaders who understand and know how to use power are more effective than those who do not or will not.

In Appendix A, we tie these descriptions of types of power, both positional and personal, to Follower Readiness Levels, Leadership Styles and the Key Power Bases upon which leaders may call to exercise power appropriately and avoid **Paradoxes of Power**.

Hersey and Kenneth Blanchard first developed Situational Leadership in the late 1960s. It is based on two key dimensions of leadership behavior: *providing direction* and *providing support*.[2] They developed a model that prescribed recommended forms of leadership behavior suited to the readiness levels of their followers. The interactive nature of leadership style and followership behaviors is key to their model.

Directive Behavior is the extent to which a leader defines roles for followers, and explains what to do and when, where and how tasks are to be accomplished.

Supportive Behavior is the extent to which a leader builds and maintains positive relations with followers, characterized by effective 2-way communication, feedback, encouragement, praise and friendly interaction.

Let's review the definitions and the relationships between *performance readiness*, *leadership style*, and the *key power bases* that typically best drives that style. We'll use the standard Hersey-Blanchard convention of "R" and "S" ratings to show levels of "Readiness of Followers" and "Style of Leadership," using 1-4 as the scales for each. This is the heart of the discussion of the application of power.

Readiness Levels
R1 = Very Unable and/or Very Unwilling
R2 = Somewhat Unable but Willing
R3 = Able but Not Fully Confident or Not Fully Enthusiastic
R4 = Very Able, Willing and Confident

Leadership Styles
S1 = Above Average Direction and Below Average Supportive Behavior
S2 = Above Average Direction and Above Average Supportive Behavior
S3 = Below Average Direction and Above Average Supportive Behavior
S4 = Below Average Direction and Below Average Supportive Behavior

Key Power Bases

Coercive Power—The Perceived Ability to Provide Negative Consequences for Not Performing
Followers at performance readiness level R1 need guidance and direction. Too much supportive behavior with people at this level who are not currently performing, may be perceived as permissive or as rewarding the lack of performance.

Connection Power—The Perceived Association of the Leader with Influential Persons or Organizations
Connection power is an important driver for "telling" (S1) and

"selling" (S2) leadership styles. Usually, followers at R1 and R2 want to avoid the sanctions or gain the favor they associate with powerful connections.

Reward Power—The Perceived Ability to Provide Things That People Would Like to Have

Reward power is enhanced if followers perceive managers as having the ability to give appropriate rewards. Followers who are unable to currently perform a certain task but are willing to make an effort (R2) are most likely to try on new behaviors if they feel increases in performance will be rewarded. Rewards may include raises, bonuses, promotions, or transfers to more desirable positions.

Legitimate Power – The Perception that the Leader has the Right to Make Decisions because of Title, Role or Position in the Organization

Legitimate power can be a useful driver for both the selling and participating leadership styles but ineffective for followers who are both unable and unwilling or insecure (R1). They may not care whether someone's title is supervisor or manager. Similarly, followers high in performance readiness (R4) are far less impressed with title or position than they are with the leader's expertise or information.

Referent Power—The Perceived Attractiveness of Interacting with the Leader

In attempting to influence people who are able but insecure or unwilling (R3), high-relationship behavior is necessary. If people have a confidence problem, the manager needs to provide encouragement. If they have a motivation problem, the manager needs to discuss and problem solve. In either case, if the manager has not taken time to build rapport, attempts to participate may be perceived as adversarial rather than helpful.

Information Power—The Perceived Access to, or Possession of Useful Information

The styles that tend to effectively influence followers at above-average performance readiness levels (R3 and R4) are participating (S3) and delegating (S4). Information power is most helpful in driving these leadership styles.

Expert Power—The Perception That the Leader Has Relevant Education, Experience and Expertise

Followers who are competent and confident require little direction or supportive behavior. They are able and willing to perform on their own. The driver for influencing these followers is expert power. With followers who are able and confidently willing (R4), leaders are more effective if they possess the expertise, skill, and knowledge that followers respect and regard as important.

In summarizing a review of the most important research relating supervisory power bases to follower satisfaction and performance, I reached the following general conclusion: Although expert and legitimate power bases appear to be the most important reasons for compliance, and expert and referent power bases tend to be strongly and consistently related to follower performance and satisfaction measures, the results are not clear enough to generalize about a best power base.[3]

Figure 1, below, relates the types of power bases I described above to the Readiness Levels of Followers. The important thing about this depiction is that it recommends or prescribes certain power bases that correspond with the follower's Readiness Level, noted as "R4" through "R1," where a follower is most prepared and motivated to perform a mission or task shown as an R4. R1 levels depict a follower who may be neither prepared nor motivated, often through no fault of their own. These followers are ill-equipped to contribute much to the power relationship, whereas an R4 may be an outstanding contributor to the relationship.

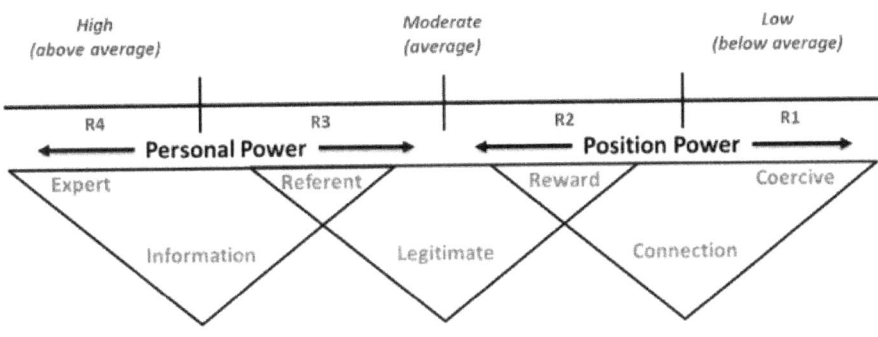

Figure 1 - Power Bases and Readiness of Followers, by Walter E. Natemeyer and Carl W. Hunt

Appendix A, "The Essentials of Power and Influence," dives much deeper into the substance and essence of human power in all its manifestations. This initial introduction provides the general overview of what power is in all types of relationships and how it works in practice. Armed with this overview, readers will be better prepared to appreciate the discussions in the essays and see for themselves how power is diverted into what we call **Paradoxes of Power**.

1. Power And Paradox

By Carl W. Hunt and Joshua M. Hunt

Defining Paradoxes of Power

I n late Spring of 2020, fellow essayist Larry Kuznar and Carl (along with Foreword author, Stuart Kauffman) co-published a post titled "Why politics is so polarized, even though Americans agree on most key issues," on the Oxford University Press Blog.[4] The post reflected on the strength of an almost 50-year old leadership theory called "The Abilene Paradox," first introduced by Professor Jerry B. Harvey, then a professor at The George Washington University. This theory and subsequent writings regarding the theme inspired our thinking about **Paradoxes of Power**.

The concept of "The Abilene Paradox" is simple: people often collectively agree to do things that none of them actually want to do. This is not for a lack of compromise, or even what's known as Groupthink.[5] The paradox Harvey described instead explains people allowing or even enabling themselves to act against their own desires. Why? Because nobody in the group is willing to voice his or her interests or overtly demonstrate disagreement with one another. Likely, there could have been total accord between the people in the group, but something about the dynamics of their interactions completely inhibited any possibility of resolution. A true paradox, indeed!

Our blog post applied the concepts of the paradox to try to explain how so many Americans in recent decades could engage in self-destructive behaviors that threaten to tear our "national fabric" to pieces. A truly paradoxical definition, "public agreement, private disagreement" is how management guru Rosabeth Moss Kanter elegantly described "The Abilene Paradox." Dr. Kanter observed that the situation is a result of private opinions rarely being expressed publicly.[6] This demonstrates a significant failure of the power relationship between leaders and followers. It also occurs within organizations which don't formally manifest leadership and followership as explicitly as a company or institution, as we describe below. Such a paradox could even be observable in a peaceful group protest that turns violent, for example.

Dr. Harvey's ideas were a way to explain how groups of people could allow themselves to collectively behave in a manner that absolutely none of them wanted: publicly agreeing while privately disagreeing. Harvey began to get leaders and followers to think about how they mismanage *agreement* as well as the more traditionally known management dilemma, *lack of agreement*. He proposed that mismanaging agreement was "a major source of organization dysfunction." In fact, according to Harvey, this type of poor management was the most significant misuse of leadership power known to exist at the time.[7] To us as writers/researchers, this seemed like a paradox worth studying to determine if it could be applied elsewhere and at what scale. As a result of that blogging exercise earlier this year and additional research, we believe that paradox situations scale all too well through every level of organization and government, particularly in the United States of America.

While much of Harvey's work reflected anecdotal observations, his "Abilene Paradox" has withstood the test of time. More importantly, his notion of paradoxes in power relationships opened the door to new thinking and the critique of what were, at their respective times, "tried-and-true" leadership techniques. For a framework sharing traditional ways of thinking about power and leadership, we included Dr. Walter E. Natemeyer's excellent and detailed summary in Appendix A, as previewed in Chapter 0.5. For those who want a more detailed understanding of how power works in almost every organizational setting, we encourage our readers to closely review this superb overview.

*Unfortunately, failures in power relationships and the resultant **Paradoxes of Power** scale all too efficiently.*

Paradoxes of Power follows Harvey's model to the degree that we challenge the so-called traditions, and that we don't present much more than anecdotal, experience-based insights to "learn the cures." We believe that human imagination and willingness to learn to succeed in new situations is still a prized asset, and good leaders and followers will work out for themselves how to apply "anti-paradox" thinking once they're aware of the existence and pitfalls of **Paradoxes of Power**. The more we can recognize and avoid power paradoxes, the more we can succeed in organizational settings. Also, we don't believe that a detailed review of every category of power failures in organizations will provide much deeper insight than already exists. Unfortunately, failures in power relationships and the resultant **Paradoxes of Power** scale all too efficiently. This essay and indeed the entire book challenge the reader to raise their own questions about their experiences in organizational life and apply the solutions proposed throughout the essays to their specific circumstances.

Jerry Harvey influenced us significantly, and as we reflected on the phenomenon of group behaviors that totally missed the mark in good decision making, we did some reflecting on our own experiences in organizations. The same principles typically applied to the way power is exercised within any type of organization. This and so many similar leader-follower behaviors observed in diverse types of groups demonstrate significant discrepancies in power relationships. Indeed, **Paradoxes of Power** abound.

After inspecting examples of the types of organizations we studied, we realized that it doesn't matter the size or the nature of the organization, community, or even nation – paradoxes seem to scale frighteningly well across the board. People often allow themselves to "climb on the bus" to a location or objective that satisfies no one, including the organization itself. Boarding the "bus to Abilene," as the good professor later called it, was socially and organizationally counterproductive, and ultimately amounted to a failure of authority and leadership power.

There is a lot more to the concept of power than its role in leadership but examining how leaders and groups succeed and fail with the exercise of power is a fair starting point to expand our study. This book is not just a recap of "The Abilene Paradox" however, because the ideas about **Paradoxes of Power** go much further.

> *...paradoxes of power occur when a person or organization exercises authority in a way that reduces the potential of the group as a whole.*

Stated in simplest terms, *paradoxes of power occur when a person or organization exercises authority in a way that reduces the potential of the group as a whole.* It diminishes or destroys the possibility for an effective power relationship between leader(s) and follower(s). When this happens, the proportion of organizational benefit to non-benefit or harm-to-others shifts so dramatically that the power relationship enters a state of contradiction, or paradox. Worse, these contradictions and paradoxes may be further aggravated by organizational issues related directly to discrimination and prejudice. We will explore some of these pernicious malfunctions in later essays.

The most important attribute of power, as a connecting feature of human relationships, is that *power is a two-way street.* Effective uses of power are based on good social relationships. There is a *wielder **of** power* and there is a *yielder **to** power*, and any given social relationship must feature both parties in balance for there to be any positive and lasting effect. The following figure shows one way to look for an objective balance in some of these relationships and demonstrates how organizations achieve paradox.

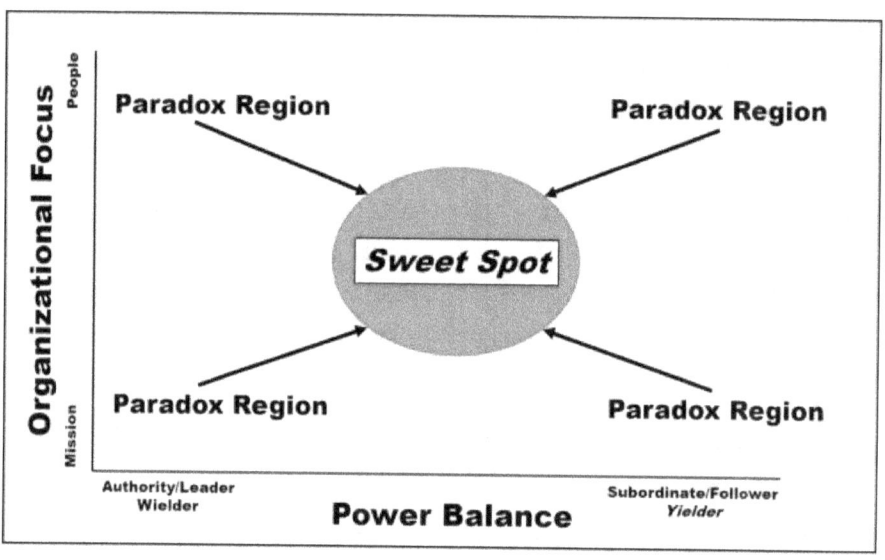

Figure 2 - The "Sweet Spot" of Balance of Power and Organizational Focus, by Carl W. Hunt

Admittedly, Figure 2 is a simplistic and incomplete way of looking for a "sweet spot" in a leader-follower social relationship. This inexact illustration points to only a couple of basic measurements: the organizational focus between mission and people, and the tendency of an organization to place more emphasis on the few or the many, often leaders and followers, respectively. These wielders and yielders either consciously enter these relationships, or they do it implicitly, but it is generally a choice, and the sum of those individual choices directly affects the success or paradox the team experiences. In short, a balanced power relationship reduces the chances for problems and increases the likelihood of success.

In either event, the illustration *does* highlight common pitfalls organizations make in relying on or even emphasizing one type of leader-follower behavior over another.[8] Let's look at an example of each "Paradox Region" (PR) and how a group may come to inhabit it. Labeling these examples as "regions" also indicates there is no single point of paradox but rather, it's a zone that is not always clearly delineated, and therefore not always easy to detect when the organization is in paradox.

An instance of the PR in the top left quadrant could include any situation where the authority or management is almost exclusively focused on the people within the organization; the mission might even be an afterthought. A student of leadership might say that a Not-For-Profit group, such as a food or utility Co-Op, could be a good example of this. In such a group, the focus is on the members and effective leadership is a secondary concern. In fact, leadership in this example is often composed of community or neighborhood volunteers with little or no training. It could be a great place to work and have fun...for a time. Eventually, the organization in this PR either becomes more mission-leader focused, or perhaps goes out of business entirely due to a lack of guidance and direction. A significant paradox in this situation is the loss of motivation of the people serving in these organizations even though the emphasis was clearly on the need and the roles the volunteers played. The group did good for the community, it just couldn't sustain that good without more effective power relationships.

The PR in the bottom left quadrant is indicative of a more autocratic management approach, where people are viewed primarily as tools to further the organization's interests. Some might suggest that the US Military is a good illustration of this type of focus, and indeed, there are times, such as a national security crisis, where "mission first" is the appropriate emphasis. Carl has served in military units that attempted to temper this mentality by using the motto "Mission first - people always," but that is a tough balance to maintain for even the most flexible of organizations. In this quadrant, followers must be very mission focused and dedicated to the purpose of the group, to continue to yield to its leader's power. The most significant paradox in this type of organization is that people are critical to the success of the mission, yet are often the most disposable of the resources available to accomplish the mission. Even if this paradox condition never fully comes to pass, leaders must guard against the perception of their followers that they are expendable.

Conversely, the upper right region might demonstrate a situation where a union or professional association has dominant control over an organization. Here, the primary concern is for the employees, perhaps even to the outright exclusion of the mission. Currently in the United States, police departments all too often serve as a poignant example of this concept. The protest events of spring-summer 2020 surrounding various instances of apparent police misconduct have led many to believe that police unions control the relationships of a community's police officers, to the exclusion of the community's overall welfare. There is a major paradox evident in this exact scenario, as the police's motto or creed is to "protect and serve." It's unlikely that this motto originally spoke to protecting and serving the police department or the union. We will examine this more closely in chapters 7 and 8.

Finally, the bottom right PR might contain an employee-owned company. It may be something like a "start-up" perhaps, where the focus initially falls strictly on the success of the group and its mission. There may be multiple leader figures, or there may be no clear leader, as power may be distributed evenly, at least initially, among the various team members. In this type of organization, both employees and "bosses" work hours and hours each day to get initial products or services out the door quickly so the organization is making money as soon as possible. Leadership, if you will, is left in the hands of the people who serve as the so-called experts. The most evident paradox in this situation is that burnout of employees, regardless of competence level, is not uncommon, and the employees leave after they've learned so much and achieved success. They take those lessons and success with them just when the original organization needs them the most.

The application of power in these types of "outer quadrant" relationships is rife with the potential for misuse or abuse of its resultant relationships. While power can produce value and do organizational good, the focus of our study falls on the challenge of overcoming these misapplications of power that produce poor individual and group behaviors. The prescriptions in the concluding parts of the essay and throughout the book focus on bringing the organization into the "Sweet Spot" that balances the power relationships between followers and leaders. This forms the basis for our further exploration of **Paradoxes of Power** and the avoidance of them in the first place.

*The people subject to an authority presumably give up their own power so that the organization collectively benefits; their individual contributions and power are squandered through **Paradoxes of Power**.*

Groups and organizations are formed to take advantage of the insights, experiences, and energies of their individual members. A **Paradox of Power** robs groups of the ability to take advantage of these valuable collected talents and efforts. The paradox significantly hinders their maximum potential. To paraphrase an important point from Walt Natemeyer's contribution to this book in Appendix A: The people subject to an authority presumably give up their own power so that the organization collectively benefits, and their individual contributions and power are squandered through paradoxes.

Here are more instances of Paradoxes of Power in a variety of settings. Note how a lack of common sense contributes to the formation and exercise of power in these circumstances.

- Kim Jong-Un, the leader of North Korea, has been the supreme leader of his people since 2011. He was only 25 years old or so when he assumed this position as the head of a nation with nuclear weapons and a massive military force. Prior to that time, he served briefly at the "slightly accelerated" rank of a four-star general in the North Korean army, with no other prior military or government service reported. He is by all accounts exceedingly unqualified, yet rules Korea with an iron fist. How can something like this be allowed to happen in any civilized nation?

- In contrast, many leaders of organizations don't want to be leaders at all, or at least recognize their lack of qualifications or experience. However, they ultimately accept the mantle of power and proceed to exercise it even though they know they are "in over their heads." They may grow used to wielding power and eventually become proficient at it, but they often lack confidence and make poor decisions in the meantime. This is paradoxical enough, yet often the organizations that appointed these leaders are reluctant to strip them of their power. Whether for fear of change or fear of criticism, they would rather stay the course than make a choice that could set things straight. Alternatively, in the example of criminal syndicates, it's just fear in and of itself that prevents the organization from making change, as the "leaders" often achieved power through violence or cleverness alone. As should be evident, paradox is strongly manifest in these situations.

- In another example, an organization may fail to adequately prepare potential leaders to take on the responsibilities of their post. This can be a result of poor screening, or due to misjudgment of the candidate's character or capabilities.

Contrary to what logic would dictate, the organization still vests power and authority in these newly minted leaders and does little or nothing to make up for the shortcomings they bring with them. Meanwhile, the entire organization crumbles around their feet. This may seem paradoxical in the extreme, yet it is frighteningly common in government, business, religion, and academia. These occurrences stem frequently from malfeasance, or other harm, from a leadership level. These practices have direct and negative effects on followers, as well as on the health of an organization as a whole. The insightful reader will be able to cite examples in all the categories mentioned above, with particular emphasis on political leaders in the United States, both past and current.

- In a different type of power paradox, sometimes leaders can't or won't share power, regardless of the suitability and maturity of their followers. There are multitudes of reasons to share power with qualified followers to achieve success and balance. So many in fact that we won't mention them here, although we urge you to consider how hard it is to "lead" even oneself in the complex world we inhabit today. Why would a leader not want to grow and nurture followers to help in innovating, managing, and ensuring the survival of the organization? Just as paradoxically, why would a mature follower want to stay in an organization that is run by an authoritarian who doesn't trust the most precious asset they have—their people?

- This next example, as well as the one that follows, relate more specifically to US politics, although other nations likely face the same issues. Politics itself is a paradox related to the reality of life in a "free" nation. Politicians run on promises to serve their constituents, despite knowing that there is no reliably effective way to keep their promises. They offer to be so in touch with their respective constituents that they can anticipate problems before they occur, yet fail to deal with those problems until they have been raised to a level at which it is often too late to holistically solve them. The paradox is that voters elect these leaders knowing full well that they cannot or will not solve their problems, at least not before it is too late to effect meaningful change. Instead, they elect them because they "like" the politicians or they want to protect a very narrow set of issues. Local communities and both state and federal policies suffer from weak, fragmented solutions that cost much more than they should and feel a lot more like afterthoughts than carefully planned out initiatives. "Rearview politics" defeats the purpose of leaders having power and influence to begin with, and failure to take proactive steps towards solutions ruins their ability to accomplish anything meaningful during their time in office. At that rate, why even run for office to begin with? If that's not paradoxical enough, the electorate returns the same failed politicians to office at the very next opportunity. There is simply no logical explanation for that.

- Another paradox related to US politics is the expectations we have for our senators, an issue that's surfaced prominently in recent years. In Federalist Paper No. 62, James Madison argued that senators would be the bridge between the states and the national government. He then doubled down on this idea in Federalist 63, describing the importance of the senate having "a national character." House members were primarily elected to directly serve their districts, while senators would offer a balance of representation that could serve the broader interests of the state that elected them. Senators would also serve the national government in the big picture issues such as tempering the passions of the house members (who represent narrower, more local constituencies) and ratifying treaties with other nations. Today, at least half of the Senate represent the interests of their members' own political parties first and foremost, and fail to act with the bigger picture in mind. Some senators, primarily on the GOP side, act more like house members, guided by the passions of their party over national or even state interests. As with the example above, voters acknowledge all of this and somehow still choose to return these individuals to office repeatedly. Somewhere along the line, Americans forgot that their *states* are stronger when their *nation* is stronger.

We decided not to specifically call out "Paradoxes of Political Power" in this book because it would take an entire multivolume set to do so. The examples above, however, demonstrate that paradoxes permeate our lives, and that power imbalances aggravate the failings that arise from them. With "Abilene" and its lessons in mind, we can choose to analyze whether these paradoxes arise from coping with disagreement, or from accommodating what we perceive to be agreement.

*The key identifier of the **Paradox of Power**: individuals yield their power to the collective, and the collective and its superior power potential fails to achieve something greater than the sum of its parts, a major objective for any organization.*

When the group takes or subjects itself to some action against their benefit, they experience one of the several regions of paradox like those we describe in Figure 2. Throughout the remainder of essays in this book, we'll examine a variety of additional sources of paradox in a variety of groups and settings where despite their origins, the people subject to authority have one thing in common: they suffer, both individually and collectively. In the key identifier (e.g., failure) of the **Paradox of Power**, individuals yield their power to the collective, and the collective and its superior power potential *neglects to achieve something greater than the sum of its parts*, a major objective for any organization.

Before moving on to mitigation and solutions to **Paradoxes of Power**, it's worth introducing the idea of *emergence*, which is covered in detail in Appendix B. Both power and paradox are emergent characteristics of all organizational relationships. Good leaders seek to harness the qualities of their followers and assemble an organization in which the group can achieve something greater than the sum of its parts. Group and collective relationships almost always produce more than first expected, and good power relationships produce emergent, more beneficial effects. Emergence may not always be a positive outcome, however, particularly when that emergence is a **Paradox of Power**.

A paradox is frequently thought of as the opposite reaction, or even a surprising outcome, to what participants would have imagined initially. A paradox is not always easy to detect, and recognition of it can be obscured by bias, experiences, lack of training or often a combination of the three. Working through this requires thought, as well as valid reasoning to overcome the flaws presented by the paradox. "The Abilene Paradox" described at the beginning of this chapter is a good case in point. Who would have imagined that literally everyone in a group would have a differing preference from the one the group ultimately selects? That doesn't seem reasonable at all, yet Harvey showed that's exactly what happens in a paradox of that nature.

Avoiding and Mitigating Paradoxes

The identification of "The Abilene Paradox" is not Jerry Harvey's only contribution to our study. He and other thoughtful writers also suggested how to *deal with* the paradox before, during, and after it is recognized.

In what he called a "Bypass [around Abilene]," Harvey identified several root causes that could be useful to understand if identified in power relationships. In other words, these causes should be recognizable to any of the players on the team and could be identified early on rather than waiting until the metaphorical "bus" gets all the way to Abilene. The same factors apply very well to any of the paradoxes we identified in the previous sections.[9]

The first factor Harvey identified dealt with assignments of blame and claims of fault, which tend to fall on everyone *except* the person who does most of the criticism. As he notes, "executives begin to assign one another to roles of victims and victimizers." This is an "irrelevant and dysfunctional" activity, because in the time it takes the team to *fail* at managing its agreements, the bus has already arrived at its destination. "All its members are victims," and it's hard to problem solve when everyone but the accuser shares the blame. Meanwhile nobody takes responsibility for anything, and progress towards a resolution all but stalls out, Harvey wrote.

A second factor speaks to the reciprocal nature of human problems in organizations. That is, both leaders and followers need each other to take the trip to Abilene. Everyone chooses to focus on the perceived conflicts among members rather than recognize areas of agreement. With an emphasis on the latter, they could have avoided the bus altogether. Instead, they feed off each other's negativity, making it difficult for any solution to present itself as practical and beneficial for the group—this is reciprocity at its worst. This is also the part of the paradox that can produce lasting damage to an organization. In this instance, good leaders will recognize the emergence of the paradox and reassess both their application of power and the styles of leadership they use. Walt Natemeyer describes these opportunities and strategies for positive change in Appendix A.

It might be normal to assume that a boss or leader should be responsible for doing something about a problem that arises in his or her group, but a third factor suggests that this isn't the case. The issue is one of accountability. The question becomes: who *is* responsible for solving the disagreements? To paraphrase Harvey, the answer is *anyone and everyone.* Each individual can step up and attempt to draw attention to the destructive direction in which the group is headed and should feel responsible and motivated to do so for everyone's benefit. Both yielders and wielders should feel empowered to suggest solutions and should recognize the consequences of encouraging further conflict. This concept speaks to the value of humility on the part of both leaders and followers in any given power relationship.

This also means members of power relationships need to prioritize their perception of disputes. Some conflicts are more serious than others, and some may not even be "real" in the sense that they are rooted in completely illogical or irrational thinking. Consider a group in which one or more members choose to use race, age or gender as a basis for a conflict which *would not exist* were it not for personal biases. The notions of racism, sexism, ageism, and gender bias, while tragically still very alive today, are outdated in the extreme; these biases are so illogical that they have no place in a modern country that claims to offer equality and freedom to its citizens. Still, they persist and create paradoxes.

> *What have we achieved in our nation's history by holding on to biases and creating legacies of the damage they've wrought?*

Think of the waste of resources, time, influence, and buildup of negative emotion that these biases have caused our nation...to protect against what? What have we achieved in our nation's history by holding on to these biases and creating legacies of the damage they've wrought? This simply can no longer be a point of argument; therefore, any group that allows one or more members to encourage conflict in this manner finds itself in a deep state of paradox. The consequence of what are phony conflicts such as what these biases represent is that the team must now spend extra time and energy to solve a problem that shouldn't have gained any traction in the first place.

Returning once again to Harvey's insights, both real problems and phony ones can be resolved through honest and objective confrontation and communication. Team members should encourage and enable each other to interact in this way. This is how groups can find the "sweet spot" depicted in the middle of our Figure 2 graphic. Phony conflict is the primary cause of *counterintuitive compromise,* a statement which is paradoxical in and of itself, yet perfectly represents the logic (or lack thereof) behind boarding the bus to Abilene.

In his advice for engaging, rather than evading the opportunities to overcome conflicts, author Parker J. Palmer discusses ways to work through the tensions that diversity and democracy present. Palmer recommends we "listen to each other openly and without fear," and work hard to understand the experiences of others that may be "radically unlike" us so that we can build empathy for their lives and how they became what they are rather than what we might want them to be. We should "welcome opportunities to participate in collective problem solving and decision-making" so that our solutions are strengthened by diverse thinking. These thoughts are key to building resilient structures whether in human relationships or in all living systems.[10]

Power relationships are two-way streets, to which both leaders and followers can contribute if the leader has the humility to recognize and leverage the followers' skills, experience, and insight.[11] Leaders can be just as unready to empower relationships as followers...another anomaly which can be easily overcome if we can learn to recognize **Paradoxes of Power**. If we can't...we may spend so much time headed towards Abilene that there's no going back.

2. An Introduction To The Essays

by Carl W. Hunt

Suppose a powerful business leader or politician asked, "Alright, so what is this **Paradox of Power** thing? Why don't you tell me about it while we're on the way up to the office?"

Here's how I might answer that:

Consider the world around us: it's messy, chaotic, context-sensitive, and constantly evolving. If we ever hope to orient ourselves, we need to understand that "the questions" are just as important as "the answers." In fact, the questions are even more important, because we can't hope to understand how things work by simple passive observation and acceptance of them.

*Let's simplify our challenge; think of a vertical line drawn at the bottom of our messy worldview. On the left side of the line is the concept of **power**. In ideal conditions, power is the potential to get things done: to attract and garner resources, and to collect and utilize tools to accomplish things. When outside forces get involved however, such as chaos, coercion, and competition, power can quickly disorient us. On the right side of the line is **success**, which must be measured somehow to prevent the exercise of power from being futile. We as humans are not the best at defining and measuring success yet, even after centuries of history to learn from and build from. Furthermore, success requires the assumption of **responsibility**, which often sounds better on paper than how it ends up working in practice. With a better understanding of power however, we can fix that.*

Responsibility for turning power into success and overcoming chaos *and other subversive forces must be a shared **obligation** between leaders and followers. The more balance there is, the more likely the outcome can be effective, repeatable, and sustainable. As the "'success" side of our imaginary line becomes more apparent, it encourages the creativity and imagination of everyone involved, and keeps the momentum going in a positive direction. And as success is achieved, it must be shared equitably, a concept which seems conspicuously absent in many political and organizational power relationships today. Those in power must always seek this balance, sharing that power and their resources to continue to accomplish objectives. This is the way we move ourselves forward through the chaotic world. Leaders are creating paradox when we fail to move forward.*

To sum things up, both leaders and followers must always have "skin in the game." As a result, responsibility and success must be shared and balanced in a way that benefits everyone. Understanding this concept is of the utmost importance when it comes to identifying and mitigating **Paradoxes of Power**, which is the goal of both our book and our blog series. Too many American organizations including government, business, academia, and religion refuse to trust their followers and to invest in them, which ironically, even paradoxically, stands to hurt the leaders as much as it does anyone else.

This Chapter 2 essay offers several thoughts. First, it serves as a bridge between the introduction of the concepts of **Paradoxes of Power** in Chapter 1 and the essays that proceed through the rest of the book. Secondly, it contextualizes the remaining essays to present a flow of ideas that describe how pervasive the use, and more to the point, misuse of power has manifested in what we still believe is the greatest nation in the history of the world. Or at least it should be, given all the advantages the United States has enjoyed in its short tenure in the unfolding of world events. I've served this nation over 40 years as a police officer, soldier and government consultant so I think I have my "skin in the game."

Finally, this essay seeks to justify why the reader should want to continue on: what our essayists have to say is important and fundamental to the success of this nation and its future generations. As the Preface notes, we "published this book to help our youngest generations in America to better understand and appreciate the role that power plays in our societal relationships at every level." If you represent one of the elder generations of America, we hope you'll "wield the power" these essays present to reinforce the ideas to your own young generations and help to make our nation the best it can be. If it helps other freedom-loving nations and their citizens, that's even better.

Chapter 3, "Who is in Charge?" is an excellent icebreaker into the real world of **Paradoxes of Power**. This essay is a hybrid of fine storytelling and keen analysis that breaks down some of the most significant challenges this or any nation in modern history has faced. From one paradox to another, this chapter tests readers to understand and at last question why America has evolved the way it has since its founding, and appreciate the kinds of changes we might make to better fulfill our destiny and employ peoples' talents, intuitions and experiences in ways that we've overlooked for too long.

Chapter 4, "The Paradoxes of Race in America" offers some of the most potent paradoxes we discuss in this book, as they are all about people, culturally and individually. This chapter, presented in powerful first-person narratives, describes challenges and situations that a nation as influential and progress-oriented as America believes itself to be, should have been resolved long ago: the paradoxes of failing to come to grips with the contributions of all our people and fully integrating every race of Americans and would-be Americans into a cohesive force for good in this country.[12] Our America has spent a great deal of blood and treasure fighting the full embrace of all our people...*all our people*...and what they have to offer our future. These first two essays are rich with **Paradoxes of Power**.

Chapter 5, "Power in the Post-Pandemic Economy" is a paradox within a paradox. Author Lawrence Kuznar in fact titles this essay, "A Tale of Two Paradoxes: Isolationism and Globalization." Larry calls on a concept that economist Brain Arthur calls "complexity economics" to kick off his essay which goes a long way towards "simplifying" what is likely to happen in the post-pandemic economy. Using rich data analysis from the Pandemic of 1918 and its effects on our economy of the century past, Larry finds revealing similarities and contrasts that help us prepare for the next version of a US economy. Paradoxes abound when it comes to interacting with our economy. Readers may want to refer to Appendix B to touch up on their understanding of complexity and emergence before tackling this chapter to ensure they get the most out of it. Some of the ensuing essays also refer to these concepts.

Chapter 6, "Human Power versus Nature's Power" is focused on much more than our country. It offers a spotlight on all humanity and our role in taking care of our home, lovingly referred to as planet earth. This essay applies to every living thing on earth, but most specifically to the select group of species that can perhaps do the most to protect this world: Americans. This includes Americans of every age and political persuasion. **Paradoxes of Power** exist everywhere when it comes to human interaction with our environment. If we don't take our leadership and power roles seriously in preserving our land, water, air and yes, every other species with which we partner in our world, we have failed both America and the rest of the world, now and throughout our remaining history. As a preview to this essay, Nature has far more power than people, and she's not afraid to use it.

Chapter 7, "Government, Politics and Education: their roles in Paradoxes of Power" is one of two most academically oriented essays in the collection. Had it not been written by two flaming academics, perhaps apologies would be in order. However, the roles of Government and Education have interacted in such distinctive ways in this country's history that the essayists felt it required a particularly objective and detached approach to describe how the interactions produced the most divisive and affective **Paradoxes of Power** we've ever experienced as a nation. The authors ask that you take the time to wade through these ponderings to better understand how power has been used and misused in these critical areas of our nation's fabric to better appreciate how to leverage the discussions in the remaining chapters to lift our nation out of the paradoxical quagmire that has engulfed the United States for far too long.

Chapter 8, "Religion and Justice as Paradoxes of Power" is the other academic essay, despite the subject containing two topics that are less about "reason" and "fact" and more about "truth" and "discovery." Larry Kuznar, my coauthor, and I felt the effects of America's founding during the throes of The Age of Enlightenment merited separate treatment from the topics of the previous essay. In this piece not only do we present some penetrating historical insights, but we also ask some questions that should expose the **Paradoxes of Power** that have long surrounded religion and justice as they have been practiced in the US since before its founding. We hope that taking the time to address these questions in the light of all the great insights from the previous essays will help us all to be both better Americans and to understand more fully how power works in our world today.

Chapter 9, "Your Power: Recognizing and Resolving Your Own Paradoxes" is the first of the closing essays we designed to pull together all the previous lessons and experiences, and to help readers orient and grow in their understanding of how power affects us all in the very trying times we have ahead of us. While the following chapter might look at the more general future of power, Chapter 9 makes it personal. In this more concise essay, Joshua and I challenge our young generation readers/leaders to reflect on the diverse topics contained within our collection of essays and find their own questions and sources for answers to tackle this new America they will soon inherit. Our greatest hope is that our young people will find meaningful new ways to avoid **Paradoxes of Power** and mitigate those that the past generations left to them to resolve.

Chapter 10, "The Future of Power" is our time to prognosticate about America's future and our individual and collective power relationships. This comprehensive essay contains the insights of our collaborating authors about the future of our nation and our power, both individual and collective.

Chapter 11, "Epilogue" is a very brief collection of our thoughts from the experiences we obtained in putting together this book. Our fellow essayists thought deeply about their lives and what they experienced to get to this point in American history, and we wanted to do their insights justice in our conclusions. The epilogue is informal and insightful, and best of all, sufficiently challenging to keep the flow going beyond the experience of reading **Paradoxes of Power**!

Finally, Appendices A and B are provided for reference in theory and science, should you need it. It's hard to get thinkers like our essayists not to ponder the scientific implications of these experiences and insights that we've provided. Please indulge our continuing quest to understand **Paradoxes of Power**...we hope you will also continue this journey with us!

3. Who Is In Charge?

by Veronica A. Mata

"**H**i, excuse me? Can you tell me who's in charge?" Several people hurried past the intern before two of them approached. One made direct eye contact and reached out to shake hands.

"I'm the colonel. Follow me." Shaking the officer's hand, the intern couldn't help but notice that the other person was holding a video camera, which was focused directly on the handshake.

A Blackhawk helicopter roared across the sky, causing the intern to flinch as the three made their way down a row of armored personnel carriers. Noticing the motion, the colonel shouted over the noise, "Ah, don't worry, Intern, you'll get used to it!" The colonel looked directly into the camera and winked as the trees swayed in the background, still in motion from the chopper's powerful departure.

When the air was quiet again, the intern attempted a proper introduction, "All due respect, the name's..."

"Nope," the colonel interrupted sharply, "for this operation, it's nicknames only. I don't care what your name is, where you're from, or what your favorite color is. Got it, *Intern*?"

"Understood, Colonel." The intern felt slightly defeated, but the feeling was quickly replaced by intrigue as the group approached an ice cream truck parked at the end of the line of the personnel carriers.

The colonel led them towards the back of the truck. The back doors were wide open, and two people were sitting in silence on the benches lining the truck. The intern noted a distinct lack of ice cream or freezer equipment. Instead, only two mysterious individuals and an assortment of rifles, pistols, grenades and knives filled the large space. As the colonel stepped into the truck, neither person stood up or saluted. The intern took note of this too and wondered what branch of the military they were in that didn't require a formal acknowledgement of rank.

Unconcerned, the colonel broke the silence. "Intern, I'd like you to meet the crew for this op. Like you, they're not military." This explained the lack of decorum. Following the colonel's hand, the intern made eye contact with the pair and nervously smiled. "This is Fortune," the colonel said, indicating the person on the left, "And the other one is Senator." The intern reached to meet their outstretched hands. "The one that's been following us is Oscar." Scooting back, camera still in hand, Oscar silently avoided the intern's attempted handshake.

"Wait, I thought we weren't using real names?" the intern said, visibly puzzled. The colonel began to answer, but Fortune was quicker.

"Allow me to explain," Fortune said, ignoring the colonel's disapproving gaze. "You see, they call me Fortune because I used to be a CEO of a Fortune 500 company. *Used to be*. Now I'm more of a *soldier of fortune*... ironically not feeling so fortunate, sitting here in this dump. But I digress. Senator was an actual US senator—that one is pretty easy to figure out. And Oscar is an Academy Award Winner for Best Director. You got some real powerful people here!"

A brief hush fell over the group as the two in the truck stood up and stretched. "Well, we're packed and ready," Senator said. "Now that the kid's here, let's go." Oscar, putting down the camera for the first time since meeting Intern, stepped into the back of the truck, followed by the colonel. Meanwhile Senator moved up to the driver's seat. Fortune put out a hand, helping

Intern in before closing the back doors. They began to drive.

The unforgiving metal benches magnified every bump and crack in the road but didn't distract from the questions bouncing around Intern's head. Nobody had spoken since they left twenty minutes ago, and Intern certainly didn't want to be the one to break the silence. Fortune was typing diligently on some version of a smartphone while the colonel slept, somehow able to rest despite the rigid surface they were seated on. Oscar had put on a bulletproof vest, a somewhat unnerving detail, and was affixing a small camera onto it.

"Hey, kid. Look this way." Oscar's commanding voice woke up the colonel, who flashed an expression of mild irritation but said nothing. Pointing the vest camera at Intern, Oscar continued, "Do you know what we're doing today?"

The intern, still surprised by Oscar's attention, hesitated but then answered, "Well...no, not really. I mean, I got a letter. A handwritten letter at that...which was a surprise. Who *writes* letters anymore? Anyway, the letter told me to come to that base because there was going to be an 'exclusive scoop' for my newspaper. I thought that was an odd phrasing. Do people still say *scoop*? Come to think of it, I actually don't even know who sent the letter. I've been assuming it was one of you. Was it? If not...who could it have been?" As the intern rambled on for an undetermined amount of time, the colonel dozed off again.

"Wow, kid. You've got a lot on your mind," Oscar said, finally interrupting Intern's stream of consciousness. "Hold that thought though! We're here!" Oscar slipped back onto the bench, pulling the camera lens away from the intern's face and pointing it towards the truck's windshield.

Following the camera, Intern noticed a large grey warehouse. As they pulled into the parking lot, the colonel woke once more and stretched into a yawn.

"Here you go," Fortune said, handing the intern a stun gun.

"I'm sorry..." Intern said inspecting the taser, "...what's this for, exactly?"

"Look," Fortune replied, "we didn't want to brief you before we actually got here, in case you might not have the stomach for this. We've got a hostage situation. Inside is the kid of some powerful world leader or something. Honestly, I wasn't paying as much attention as I probably should have been. But hey, they said they needed me and I'm here. I'm a patriot, too, you know."
"Not very diplomatic," Senator teased, parking the truck. "But not wrong. The hostage is why we're all here. Although for some of us, doing what's right is more of a motive than the money."

The intern's mouth was dry from hanging open during the others' explanation. The senator pulled a flask from the glove compartment and handed it to the intern. "Just a little," Senator cautioned. Intern unscrewed the lid and took a drink. The whiskey was strong, but the burn brought the intern back to reality and the moisture restored the ability to talk.

"Alright, but that still doesn't answer my question. Why do I need *this*?" the intern wiggled the stun gun. "Am I going in there with you?"

"Hell no!" the colonel said with a deep laugh, "You'll be standing outside just in case, you know, if somebody gets out."

"Which they never do," Oscar boldly interrupted, fixing cameras to the additional vests that had been distributed during the conversation.

"Which they never do," the colonel repeated, calmly.

"Well, alright, a bit cocky, but fine...." Intern muttered, realizing it was too late to back out now.

Fortune popped open the truck's back door and hopped out. Colonel, Oscar, and Senator followed suit. Intern, still in some shock, slowly stepped down, taking a moment to let the vivid reality of the situation sink in.

Moving towards the side of truck, the intern saw that the others were huddled, whispering to each other. The hushed discussion concluded with a group handshake, and the four walked over to address the intern.

"Stand by that door." The colonel pointed to the spot.

"And don't forget to *use* that if someone tries to attack you," Fortune gestured vigorously towards the stun gun in the intern's hand.

"Just don't do anything stupid," Oscar gave the intern a quick smile.

"You're gonna be fine. Remember that you're mainly here to observe and report," Senator said, giving the intern a reassuring pat on the shoulder. "We didn't want to get you involved in the action if it could be avoided but having the extra set of hands is just too helpful to pass up."

The four adjusted their equipment and weaponry as they aligned in a diamond formation, with the colonel taking the lead. Now apparently ready, they moved toward the door. Keeping as far back as possible, the intern heard one of them shout, "Let's go!"

As Oscar kicked in the door, Senator tossed in a smoke grenade. Colonel entered first with Fortune trailing behind. Nobody closed the door, allowing the smoke to pour out into the parking lot. The intern, hearing no gunfire, ran to the door and looked down a now empty hallway. The four were gone.

The intern took the moment to orient, leaning up against the wall for what felt like only a split second before the sharp sound of a gunshot tore through the air. Intern straightened up and looked into the doorway again, taking care to remain as covered as possible.

"Ah! This is nuts! I can't just stand out here," Intern thought as another shot rang through the floor above. *"Come on! Let's go! You got this!"* The smoke had cleared, and Intern took several deep breaths. Not allowing another moment for rational thought to creep in, Intern entered, running straight down the hallway, which quickly darkened as the door faded into the background. Intern found a set of stairs and ascended, trying hard to ignore several bodies that occupied various positions on the floor. There wasn't enough visible trauma to be sure the victims were dead, but thankfully none of them belonged to the team.

Moving farther up the stairway, Intern spotted the entrance to a new hallway and was immediately greeted by the sight of the colonel's right boot making hard contact on the chest of a suited figure. The man almost appeared to defy gravity as he floated down the corridor propelled by the forceful kick. The flight ended abruptly as the body met a wall and crumbled into a heap on the floor. Cautiously peering into the hallway, Intern saw Fortune engaged in unarmed combat with another suited stranger. The intern had taken just enough time to study the stun gun to understand how to arm it and engaged the charge switch before rushing forward.

As the intern charged up behind Fortune's assailant, Fortune and he made brief eye contact. Without thinking, Intern pressed the charged stun gun to the back of the man who was unknowingly trapped between them. Intern could feel the target's body quiver and seize before dropping to the ground, unconscious.

"Woah! Kid, what are you doing up here?" Fortune shouted, irritated but impressed.

Before Intern could answer, they heard Oscar shout from the end of hall, "We've got him!" Senator appeared from around a corner with Oscar, and on their heels a terrified looking young man who could only be the hostage. Fortune pushed Intern in the same direction as the trio passed, headed for the stairs. The colonel followed behind, releasing another smoke grenade as several armed figures rounded the corner from where the hostage had just come.

As they descended towards the ground level, two of the previously incapacitated bodies awakened and greeted them halfway up the last flight of stairs, batons in hand. Everyone paused, each party seemingly taken aback by the sudden appearance of the other. Quickly shoving the hostage closer to Oscar and the colonel, Fortune drew a machete from a back holster as Senator pulled out two long knives from unseen sheaths. The two tightened their grips simultaneously as the assailants lunged forward.

The clashing of metal baton and blade reverberated sharply off the stairway's concrete walls. Fortune deftly maneuvered the machete to block, but never sliced or stabbed at the enemy. One final forceful blow to the head with the machete handle finally ended the fight. Whether or not that killed the attacker, Intern couldn't know, but there was hardly time to worry about that now. In the same moment, the senator executed a similar technique, blocking several oncoming blows before bringing the pommels of both knives together on the attacker's temples. With both enemies down, the group made their way down the remaining stairs and back out the initial hallway.

The huffing of their breath was the only audible sound as the group exited the building and made their way to the truck. Senator jumped in first taking the driver's seat again as the others quickly made their way in. Intern took the initiative to hop in after Senator, helping Fortune to pull the hostage in next. Senator started the engine and smashed the gas pedal, giving the colonel just enough time to close the doors before the truck careened out of the parking lot into the street.

"Damn...that feeling never goes away! I think we got some incredible footage, too!" Oscar repeatedly punched the air.

"How ya doing back there?" Senator asked as the rest of the crew inspected the hostage for injuries.

Visibly shaken but apparently unharmed, the hostage replied, "Grateful to be alive...," before launching into the tale of his capture and imprisonment at the compound. As he spoke, Intern's mind drifted back to the confounding questions from earlier.

Abruptly interrupting the conversation, the Intern asked, "Why am I here?" a question that was greeted by silence accompanied by confusion, mostly on the part of the hostage. "Is it to write about this guy being okay? Because that's great and all, but there's another story here too, and it's got me rattled. Just who the hell are you guys? Who's actually in charge here, and who has the authority to answer these questions for me? I was assuming it was the colonel, but who could say after what I saw today?" The intern was becoming visibly frustrated with the lack of explanation presented so far.

It was the colonel who finally answered, "We're sorry for the lack of disclosure. You're correct in saying that you're here 'to write about this guy being okay,' which is a big story, because he's a very important guy. These classified operations are tough. Covering them requires a certain degree of subtlety, and your employers seemed to think you were the best fit for this job. Beyond that, I really can't speculate on why *you* are here, but *you* certainly were the right person for the job. Your help today may well have bought us the time we needed to get out of there without casualties."

"As far as who's in charge," Senator chimed in, "that's a little more difficult to answer. In some ways, nobody is in charge. In other ways, we're *all* in charge. We all come from positions of power, but in this group that doesn't matter so much."

"What matters is that we work together as a team."

"We support each other," Oscar interjected. "Even Fortune,"

Oscar waved a dismissive hand in Fortune's direction, "who just claims to be 'here for the money.'" Fortune and Oscar both laughed.

"Who did *you* think was in charge?" Fortune asked, finally speaking up.

Before the intern could answer, the truck slowed to a stop, and Oscar flung open the back doors to reveal an elderly couple standing, clutching each other in front of a black sedan. Helping the hostage down from the back, Fortune led him to his parents, who had waited so long, without news, for his rescue. Crying, the three embraced each other. As Senator and the colonel began removing the tactical equipment from each team member, Intern moved to the edge of the truck and sat, watching the emotional reunion unfold. Intern remained seated, even as the four others went to shake hands with each parent, many of those handshakes turning quickly into grateful hugs laden with words of immeasurable gratitude.

They all gave gentle smiles to the parents as they parted ways, waving the intern towards them. Thanks and congratulations were exchanged, and the intern left that place with a new understanding of the importance of teamwork, regardless of each individual's respective status. The Intern hoped this wasn't the last time she would get to spend time with that incredible group of women.

As you read that story, before you got to the last paragraph, I'd like you to be honest in answering some questions: First, how did you picture each of those characters? Did you imagine that they were men, or women? Why? Did you think that they were *all* men, or that they could *all* be women? Perhaps a mix of both? Finally, would it surprise you to learn that three of the five were women of color? *Be honest with yourself.*

◆ ◆ ◆

This chapter of **Paradoxes of Power** is a thought experiment, designed to challenge our perception of who "should" occupy positions of power and how those people "should" appear. While it's possible that you didn't consider this as you read the story, it seems far more reasonable to assume that you pictured the characters in some form or fashion, even if you did so subconsciously.

Regardless of your individual expectations, it's important to understand that the answer is that *there is no right answer*. Being in a position of power and engaging in acts of heroism are non-exclusive, and there is no reason why a person doing either should have to be a certain gender or look a certain way.

Our heroes could have just as easily been men, or a mix of both men and women; however, I chose women because I wanted this chapter to have a specific emphasis on one of the *longest standing* **Paradoxes of Power** *to have ever existed*: the idea that women should be treated or viewed as being non-equal to men.

Here's another exercise. Without looking anything up, please consider the following prompts:

1. Can you name a female military general or admiral, or even colonel or captain?

This is admittedly a tough opener, as this sort of thing isn't always considered "common knowledge." So, let's try another:

2. Can you name a female film director?

Maybe a little easier, but probably still tough for a lot of folks.

3. Can you think of a female corporate CEO? In contrast, how quickly would you be able to name a male CEO?

People like Steve Jobs, Elon Musk, and Jeff Bezos are familiar to almost every American of every age group. So why is it so difficult to come up with even one powerful woman in the world of business?

4. Finally, can you name a female senator? If you can't, how about just a prominent female politician?

That last one should be the easiest of the bunch, but the undeniable fact is that *none of them should be difficult.* The idea that those questions are in any way challenging is a perfect example of how normal this power paradox has become in the United States. Worse, it's rarely considered any sort of a paradox in America, but it should be.

Viewing women as anything other than equal to men is one of the most confusing paradoxes to have emerged from human history. It has no basis in logic, reason, or any form of rational sense, regardless of how you look at it, yet it continues to affect nearly every facet of our society today.

Let's take another look at the five female leads from our story. If the characters represented accurate reflections of American society, this is how the numbers would look:

- 100% of **one** character of the main four heroines would be a senator. (Slightly less than **one** of the characters would be a member of the House of Representatives; there are 25 women senators and 102 women members of the House; by the way, that's just in the national legislature...state and local governing bodies can be even less well-represented, depending on region...let's hear it for Nevada in 2019.)[13]

- Just over a third (37%) of **one** character would be a CEO of a Fortune 500 Company. (UPS, GM, Best Buy).[14]

- About a tenth (11%) of **one** character would be an active four-star general (GEN Maryanne Miller, US Army).[15]

- Less than a tenth (7%) of **one** character would be an Oscar Award Winner for Best Director (Katheryn Bigelow)[16]

These depressing statistics suggest that women are a distinct minority in the United States. In numerous cases they are an extreme minority in many prominent facets of culture, the workplace, the military, and government in the United States. Ironically, in this country women are the literal majority: there are "165.92 million women in the United States, compared to 159.41 million men,"[17] and this trend is expected to continue for the foreseeable future. This is where the second aspect of our paradox lies:

If women are the majority by approximately 6.51 million in this country (meaning we represent 51% of the population), why do we only hold *25% percent of the Senate* and *23% of the House?* Only *a quarter or less* of our congresspeople are *actually representing women* (although they would likely claim to represent all of their constituents, regardless of gender).

Why has only *1 of 72* directors to win an Oscar for Best Director been a woman?

Why do we have only one active female four-star flag officer in the military?

Why is the highest historical percentage of female Fortune 500 CEOs only 7.4%? (The one slightly uplifting statistic to come out of 2020).

These numbers are staggering and paint a grim picture of how pervasive this **Paradox of Power** has been in our country...for a very long time. Extending the disparity further, we can include racial demographics in our analysis, which shrinks our already problematic numbers even more. Of the women "in power" mentioned above, General Maryanne Miller and director Katheryn Bigelow are both Caucasians. Furthermore, *there are no Black, Latina, Asian, or Native female CEOs on the Fortune 500 list.*[18]

And this doesn't even begin to address the wage gap between

women and men (or Caucasian women and women of color).[19] On average, for every dollar paid to a man:

- $0.82 is paid to a Caucasian woman

- $0.62 is paid to a Black woman

- $0.61 is paid to a Native Hawaiian and Pacific Islander woman

- $0.57 is paid to a Native American woman

- $0.54 is paid to a Latinx woman.

The one silver lining to all of this is that on average, an Asian woman is paid 90 cents for every dollar paid to a man,[20] suggesting that there is hope.

Taking all of this into consideration, if women represent at least 51% of the population, we should logically represent around that same percentage of each sector of society. Whether it's government, media, business, education, science, or any other organization at any level, approximately half of the "people in power" should reasonably be women. And if we assume the "rule of majority" is also responsible for the difference in pay between genders, it would also be logical to assume that if anyone were paid more, *it should be women.*

It's all enough to make me wonder: if women are literally the majority, why can't we just *overthrow the patriarchy?* I suppose it's because this kind of thinking can be problematic. "Fighting fire with fire" is often viewed as "extreme" and "irrational" in the United States, regardless of the justification, and this paradoxical perspective usually doesn't allow for much to get accomplished. Instead, like Michelle Obama says, "When they go low, we go high."[21]

Alas, if only it were that easy. Here is yet another **Paradox of Power** that women are subject to: If women banned together, listened and acknowledged each other, as well as supported one another, we wouldn't have the decisions that impact us made by anyone *but* us. We may not all agree on how we feel about abortion, women's sexual activity, and birth control, but those are discussions that should be had *by women*, not the 75% of *male* US senators or the 77% of *male* US representatives. Anything that involves women's rights, women's health, and anything about a woman's body *should be decided by women*.

If we flipped the script, imagine how men would feel if women made the decisions that controlled access to things like vasectomies, condoms, male enhancement drugs, or even physique enhancing supplements? Personally, I'll never know, because I will never understand what it means to live the life of a man, but I imagine the response would not be pretty. If history is any indicator, there would likely be violent rebellion involved, and "my body my choice" would be cast in a dramatically different light.

If you are not a woman, you *should not decide what is right for women*, whether it's health, safety, or general human rights. Taking it a step further, I will never understand what it means to be a trans-woman, a Black woman, or an immigrant woman, which means I have no right to put my two cents in to what I think is "best" for people in those demographics. It does *not* however mean that I will stop fighting for their representation too, because *we are all in this together*. As an oppressed and underrepresented group, we need to listen to and support fellow groups who are similarly oppressed and underrepresented. After all, how can we say we should have more power or rights when the same won't be offered to members of minorities or other sexual orientations? *It's not enough to think only of ourselves*.

For me, the opening narrative feels like an idealistic fantasy world, even though I'm the one who wrote it. My dream world if you will. Not the hostage situation, of course, but a world where any given person can read a story with an open mind and think: perhaps the character is male, female, trans, non-binary. Perhaps it doesn't even matter, although that would assume that we live in a world where representation is so incredibly equitable that it doesn't need to be granted, acknowledged, or made the major defining characteristic for any person, which is tragically nowhere near reality.

Despite our equally lengthy existence on this Earth, women are only very recently reaching greater positions of power. So recently, in fact, that there is still a need to use the identifier "female" when talking about it. There should never be a need to go out of our way to use gender as an identifier, especially to characterize a person in power. Don't get me wrong; any achievement a woman makes in any field or position of power should be celebrated. But when the celebration of a position of power earned is instead overshadowed by the label of "First Female" or "Only Female," it often diminishes the achievement and causes others to question the validity of it. People, especially Americans, love to try and rationalize the accomplishments of others as a means to feel better about their own lack thereof.

Sadly, the first conclusion many people make when hearing about a woman or person of color achieving a goal or position is something along the lines of:

"Oh, well she only got that award because she's a woman."

"That guy wouldn't have gotten the job if he wasn't Black. The company just wanted diversity."

"There's no way she would have gotten that scholarship if she wasn't Latina."

This paradoxical "logic" follows unfortunate precedents that have been set by the **Paradoxes of Power** we've discussed in this chapter, as well as others we'll talk about through the remainder of the book.

To my fellow femmes and to anyone else who is underrepresented, we *cannot wait* for someone else to hand us our rights or to speak up for us. *We need to keep fighting for our place at the table*. This means we not only support each other in legislature, but our fellow business leaders and owners, creators, directors, military personnel, and governmental leaders. If you're in a position of power, push others to strive for the same. Seek the representation we so desperately need. *It is our duty as humans to be inclusive.*

Growing up, I was very fortunate to have powerful female role models. From my mother, to my grandmother, my aunt, my mother-in-law, the leadership both in high school marching band and in my work. From my friends, to professors, and celebrities in media and politics. But getting the opportunity to idolize so few is not good enough. We need names of powerful women, CEOs, directors, military flag officers (generals and admirals), senators, and beyond to be on the minds of everyone, always.

I'd like to leave you with some powerful and inspiring words from some of the strong women I look up to.

"That story with all the highs and lows, and what seems so ordinary and what seems like nothing to you, is your power." - Michelle Obama

"I'm a grown woman. I can do whatever I want." - Beyonce Knowles

"Having a daughter does not make a man decent. Having a wife does not make a decent man. Treating people with dignity and respect makes a decent man... I want to thank [Senator Yoho] for showing the world that you can be a powerful man and accost women. You can have daughters and accost women without remorse. You can be married and accost women." - Alexandria Ocasio-Cortez

"So if you fight like a girl, cry like a girl...If you feel like a girl, then you real like a girl...Do your thing, run the whole damn world." - Lizzo

4. The Paradoxes Of Race In America

Editor's Note: This chapter consists of a series of shorter essays that capture specific views and distinctive insights of the authors. The editors were fortunate to find such diversity and breadth of life and professional experience in the presentations of these authors.

Essay 4.1: Why I'm Hopeful in the "Race" for Power...More Thoughts and Experiences Since the George Floyd Murder[22]

by Dennis Greene, Colonel, United States Air Force (retired), August 1, 2020

George Floyd was murdered just over two months ago on Memorial Day, May 25th, in the year of our Lord, 2020. He died a martyr. It had to happen. We know the story. We know the facts. He was murdered under the knee of an officer sworn to serve and protect him. George Floyd is dead, murdered over a supposedly counterfeit $20.00 bill, which he likely did not know was counterfeit. George Floyd is dead, murdered under the collective knee of a system rigged against him, saddled with the presumption of guilt by responding officers, completely lacking due process.

Well, Do We Really Know all the Facts?

<u>Fact:</u> Since George Floyd's murder, the Black Lives Matter (BLM) movement grew in a significant way, exposing lies and speaking truth to power. Simply put, BLM highlights police brutality against communities and persons of color while promoting social justice for everyone in the community.

Fact: Whenever civil rights struggles one step forward, backlash tries dragging progress two steps backward. Backlash is both overt and subtle. Eddie Glaude, Jr. notes in his recent book, *Begin Again*, that "(t)he word backlash covers in a cloak of innocence white fears and the politics that exploits them. Those fears throw us back into the pit and make tar babies of us all."[23]

Fact: "All lives matter" is racist backlash to the BLM movement, whether intentional or not. The focus is not on Whites. The focus is on the Black community at large.

Fact: A large swath of Whites and White America now embrace BLM, defying backlash.

Fact: *"Power concedes nothing without a demand. It never did and it never will. Find out just what any people will quietly submit to and you have found out the exact measure of injustice and wrong which will be imposed upon them, and these will continue till they are resisted with either words or blows, or with both."* Frederick Douglass, 1857.[24]

Who am I to deduce these facts? I am a Black Man, born in the 1950s, reared in Savannah, Georgia in the 1960s and 1970s, who drank from Negro Only water fountains; who used Negro Only public restrooms and facilities; who attended racially segregated public schools until halfway through 6th grade; who grew up "on the other side of the tracks" until moving to the White Savannah suburbs as a young teen only to personally endure blockbusting; who withstood sustained violence and physical attacks from many of the neighbors who remained; who was forced to fight on the school bus on a regular basis; and who escaped death on two occasions by gun carrying derelicts who surrounded my home, demanding that I (the one they called "n****r") come out to be shot.

The media might have us think some in the South still think of those times of my youth and upbringing as the "good old days," but as Glaude writes "(w)e have to tell a different story about who we are (by way of an honest encounter with our past) that challenges the repetition of myths and legends in the guise of nostalgia for simpler times."[25] Through the Black Lives Matter movement, these myths and legends are finally being exposed by tragedies such as the death of George Floyd and so many others, and it finally looks like it's time for America to move forward.

I am also a proud American, who served this country for 40 years, 30 of which were in uniform, as well as the son of a Pentecostal Holiness Pastor, who is not my father, but my mother. I am the grandson of a local Civil Rights leader, whose grandmother taught Black voters how to pass poll tests and who marched with Dr. Martin Luther King, Jr. I served as an Air Force Military Police Chief, who from scratch built and commanded the first Reserve Security Forces unit in Air Force Space Command history; whose troops were among the first to deploy to the Afghanistan conflict; who inherited several bad cops that I eventually dismissed, enduring slander, lies and several empty Congressional inquiries; who, during the time commanding this unit, was pulled over for not signaling a lane change on an empty road, while driving a top-down convertible and wearing gym gear, with a few gold chains around my neck.

Yes, Glaude is right. We have a lot of myths and legends to challenge.

What I've Learned Since George Floyd's Murder

I've learned how deeply the power of racist aggression and racist micro-aggressions savaged my soul, releasing decades of hurt, pain and flowing tears. Good actors cry on demand, something I could not do until now. Today's thoughts cause tears from a bruised soul, and therefore, I'm now better able to act both literally and figuratively.

I've learned I can be both vulnerable and strong. Vulnerable enough to open my soul, yet strong enough to speak my peace.

I've learned that in policing, a community partner is the neighbor that contributes to its welfare. If not, the police act more like the colonizer. The police were not George Floyd's partner. I've heard counter arguments for law and order, however, law and order cannot be forced by bullying those whom police protect and serve through a so called warrior mentality. Strong and permanent community policing cultures must prevail.

Speaking to culture, I've learned we need White BLM leadership to join in, because the load is too heavy for only victims to lift. Going back to Glaude and to one of his many quotes from James Baldwin: "'Color,' as (Baldwin) wrote in 1963, 'is not a human or personal reality; it is a political reality.' Color does not say, once and for all, who we are and who we will forever be, nor does it accord anyone a different moral standing because they happen to be one color as opposed to another."[26] BLM leadership that includes members of all communities will only make it stronger, less political and more personal.

I've learned to speak to Whites about White privilege, by first explaining that the roots of White privilege believes the playing field is somewhat level and mostly colorblind, when it is obviously not, and by explaining more subtly that their sincere requests for my input on race burdens me, the victim, to perhaps have to teach prior perpetrators who yielded power over me. Nonetheless, this is teaching I will gladly do, teaching that I must do.

What Happened Since the Murder and Why I'm Hopeful

As I noted above, a large swath of Whites and White America now embrace BLM, defying backlash. This gives me hope. Hope gives me power.

Confederate flags and statutes have fallen. Racist symbols are being abolished. This gives me hope. Hope gives me power.

We speak about race in casual talk feeling less awkward than before. This gives me hope. Hope gives me power.

The world better understands Martin Luther King's (MLK) famous quote, "the arc of the moral universe is long, but bends towards justice."[27] This gives me hope. Hope gives me power.

We recently lost Reverend C.T. Vivian, a humble civil rights leader and MLK lieutenant, who said, "leadership is found in the action to defeat that which would defeat you. You are made by the struggles you choose."[28] Born July 30, 1924, he passed July 17, 2020. Rest in the peace of the Lord. You are a guiding light to many and a man of extraordinarily great power.

On the very same day, we lost Congressman John Robert Lewis, another MLK lieutenant who at the age of 25 almost died from a cracked, bloody skull in 1965, while leading a peaceful voting rights march across the Edmund Pettus bridge from Selma to Montgomery. He was clubbed by state police who were authorized by Alabama Governor George Wallace. Lewis told us to pursue "good trouble." "Never give up. Never give in. Never become hostile. Hate is too big a burden to bear."[29] Born February 21, 1940, passed July 17, 2020. Rest in the peace of the Lord. You are a founding father of justice in our nation and a man of extraordinarily great power.

Power Warning Signs

Be aware of those in power prostituting America's bedrock rule of law, conflating cronyism with justice. As the title of this book says, these are **Paradoxes of Power**...abuse and misuse of the critical power relationships that all people, organizations and nations require to function effectively.

Be aware of voter suppression, led and inspired by our current Commander in Chief, creating false illusions of mail fraud among a glut of unsavory tactics. Voting remains our best force against injustice. We cannot let suppression rob our power. In fact, informed voting may be the best way to mitigate these electoral-level **Paradoxes of Power** described throughout this book.

Be aware of virtue signaling, meaning those in power pretending to show concern to gain Black and Brown votes with intent to backslide. Actions speak louder than words.

There are many, many more warnings to heed to avoid the paradoxes before they even crop up, but I trust you get the picture.

So, I Close with a Realtime Story of Civil Rights Power Backlash

I am honored to serve as Executive Director of the Denver Technological Center (DTC)/Greenwood Village (GV) Chamber of Commerce, a non-profit organization working with the City of Greenwood Village located in an affluent south metro Denver suburb, ranked in the top 30 American economic zones.

On June 19, 2020, Colorado Governor Jared Polis signed Senate Bill 217 into law, the Enhance Law Enforcement Integrity Act, regulating police actions across the state: addressing use of deadly force, standardizing data collection, outlining partner intervention expectations when a teammate cop is knowingly doing wrong, mandating body cameras, outlawing choke holds, metering use of tear gas during demonstrations, allowing officers to be sued in their individual capacities, and mandating prosecutors and grand juries release information in a timely manner.

A handful of GV police officers threatened to quit because of the new law. GV City Council responded by unanimously passing a resolution to always side with their officers and promised to pay any fines regulated against them, nullifying the meat of the law.

A peaceful protest ensued, led by a crew of young people from the local Cherry Creek High School, carrying handmade BLM signs. The city responded by placing a snowplow in front of City Hall. The next day, public supporters held a drive-by parade for the GV police force, who lined along the street waving as cars passed displaying American flags, snowplow nowhere in sight. A few days later, the GV City Council voted cash bonuses for the police force.

I shared my opposition with our Chamber City Council representative face-to-face, describing their actions as backlash. Outside legislators are attempting to bring GV into compliance, to no avail as of this writing. The Colorado State Senate vows, when back in session January 2021, to close all loopholes that unfortunately occurred, giving local communities unintended power when they passed the original law.

Despite this, GV remains steadfast in their position, citing constituent desires, making the front page of the Denver Post while leading local TV news night after night. As of today, GV moved their City Council meetings online, stating safety concerns.

I have offered to stand with GV should they reverse course. I shared my original article with our GV Chamber representative long before they took these actions and they have my phone number.[30] Although I'm not optimistic today, in remembrance of Congressman Lewis, I will continue my quest for GV to change. I will not give up. I will not give in. I will not become hostile.

This is perhaps a perfect example of controlled hallucination, meaning seeing the same thing and reaching opposite conclusions on what we saw. The legislation is not anti-police, but pro-civil rights, and as I mentioned above, whenever civil rights struggles one step forward, backlash tries dragging progress two steps backward. The GV Council reaction seems another example of a **Paradox of Power**.

The questions are how and why? The answers could provide a template of how to effectively move forward. Finding solutions will require powers of wisdom and love, rather than **Paradoxes of Power**.

Wisdom is seeing wins and losses before they happen, and love is the substance of justice. In the wisdom of Congressman Lewis, it's time for some "good trouble," and it's time to have it now to achieve one nation, under God, indivisible, with liberty and justice for all.

The struggle continues.

How Can You Best Help?

In closing, please listen, engage and believe Black Americans and Black America. We, as Black Americans, are individuals. Black America is the world in which we live. You cannot help one without helping the other. "America must listen to its wounds. It will tell us where to look for hope." – Reverend William Barber[31]

Listen with empathy, not sympathy. Listen with intent to understand. Be mindful that our words may not roll off our tongues in a way you are accustomed to.

Engage now; perfection is not the goal, movement is.

Believe what we have to say. Especially believe Black men when traditional White society is tempted to believe otherwise. Create safe havens.

Understand this is a unique time in history to make demands for permanent change.

Please know that your silence is complicit.

Fight for full economic equality for all Americans. The playing field is not level. Help to level it. Fight for equal opportunity, and don't confuse this with equal outcomes. Remember, according to Nelson Mandela, "It's the oppressor who defines the nature of the struggle."[32]

Reform our police departments. Believe Black Americans when we say systemic policing problems exist. Having been one, police chiefs know specifically who and where their problems lie. Remove chiefs not committed to change. Commit to removing them now. Support and fully empower those who do.

I think of my time in South Africa as a US Air Force Air War College student in 2002. The thesis of my research project centered on the post-Apartheid decade since 1992. I sat next to a White South African businessman on a flight from Johannesburg to Cape Town and asked his thoughts on their reforms. I shared my amazement with how far their nation had come in such a short time. He said they had to come together, or they would not have a nation. I asked him how. He said, "Truth and Reconciliation." Google it. After 400+ years of pain, America still lacks Truth and Reconciliation. It is time we have it now.

Essay 4.2 - What do we do now?

by Marc Hill

This is How It Is

"If you see something that is not right, not fair, not just, you have a moral obligation to do something about it." - John Lewis.[33] That quote rings out even more truly now than it did when the words were first spoken. As I sit here writing this at 2:30 in the morning, I consider what living in America as a black man is actually all about. Names come to mind as I think: Elijah McClain, George Floyd, Breonna Taylor, Atatiana Jefferson, Stephon Clark, Philando Castille, Eric Garner, Tamir Rice, Michael Brown...the list goes on and on. Some of the names you may know, others you may not have heard of, but all of them serve as stark reminders that "freedom" and "equality" are grossly unbalanced in this country.

The fact is, about 1 in 1,000 black men and boys in America can expect to die at the hands of police in our current "justice" system.[34] That makes them 2.5 times more likely than white men and boys to die during any given encounter with the police. Please ask yourself, "How has this become the norm in the "land of the free" and "home of the brave?" How have the statistics of black men and women being killed by police officers on a regular basis not become alarming to more people?

To answer those questions, I think we need to look at the paradoxical "out of sight out of mind" mentality that many Americans have adopted in recent years. Believing that bad things can't be happening because you are not personally aware of them or affected by them is not only completely nonsensical, but entirely selfish. The unfortunate logic that seems to follow "out of sight out of mind" is that "silence is the best answer," and that silence speaks volumes.

Let's call out a harsh reality: in the 2020 COVID-19 pandemic, there are hundreds of thousands of Americans who would choose to protest having to wear a mask to *prevent the spread of a deadly virus*, than take a stand against police brutality, systemic racism, and openly fascist political sentiments that are expressed all over the country. In a book about power paradoxes, you need look no further than people using the power of their voices to support a selfish, self-destructive mentality because they believe it infringes on their rights and freedoms, while there are Americans whose literal rights and freedoms are being oppressed on a daily basis. Ironically, these violated rights and freedoms are the same as those that the grandparents of these ignorant individuals fought in wars to protect. The irony is palpable; if having to wear a mask to protect other people enrages you but the sight of a cop's boot on an innocent young man's throat doesn't, you definitely need to check your priorities.

Another problem that stems from "out of sight out of mind" is that it encourages a dangerously biased "normal" today.

The following conversations are all too commonplace among people who don't feel affected:

"Ah well, he probably had it coming."

"He was just in the wrong place at the wrong time, that's all."

"He shouldn't have fought back, that's why he was killed."

"Why was he selling loose cigarettes on the street, anyway?"

"Well I heard he had a rap sheet a mile long, so…"

The conversations we need to be having are those that go like this:

"That cop acted as judge, jury, and executioner on a citizen he was sworn by oath to protect and serve."

"Take your knee off his throat, he's a human being not an animal."

"If he had been white, he wouldn't have been treated like that."

"Unreasonable force based on discriminatory profiling should be illegal."

While these talks do happen, they don't happen nearly enough, and this is what must come to pass in America. From the very beginning, "the system" was simultaneously set up *for the people* but *against people of color*, and it doesn't get much more paradoxical than that. The belief that any person is less free or less deserving of freedom because of their biological appearance is insane at the most fundamental levels. From the Native Americans, Chinese or Japanese in World War 2, LatinX immigrants who have come here for a better life, and Black Americans who have chosen to make this country home, the system has been put in place for these cultures to fail. But do we fail? No. We keep our heads high, even after dealing with the atrocities we have grappled with in the past. We keep moving forward, one foot in front of the other, until the day we are all thought of as equal.

Now, my experience as a young, Millennial black male today is not the same as that of my parents, grandparents, and great-grandparents. It was a different time for them, but some things never change; I've had to deal with racism from police, in school, and even on a day-to-day basis in society. Is it as prevalent or widespread as it was back in my parents' day? Four years ago, I might have said "No," but Trump coming into power in America was an unexpected twist in the story. When you take a country that has historically had immense struggles in allowing for equality and throw in a leader who has no qualms about being xenophobic, racist, openly sexist, and objectively immoral, you embolden those who share those sentiments to emerge from hiding. The scariest part? Those people could have been anywhere. It could be someone you knew and talked to for years, from a seemingly friendly neighbor to a previously supportive relative. Whatever the case, once Trump was elected these people came out in droves.

Let's talk about some truly terrifying scenarios that have played out across America. Think back to that friendly neighbor; the new administration took over, and just weeks later a confederate flag appeared in one of his windows. He doesn't wave to you anymore, and you find that he spends an uncomfortable amount of time staring at you when he sees you from a distance. He has even taken recordings of you on his phone, thinking that you can't tell he's doing it. Down the street, a woman who has been a longstanding member of your neighborhood's HOA introduces the idea that you and others in the community have been unsavory additions, and that you don't belong there. One evening, you're out walking your dog, and that same woman calls the police because you happened to walk by her house and she thought you looked suspicious and threatening when you smiled and waved to her. After that, you find that the police drive through your neighborhood a lot more frequently than they used to, and they seem to always slow down when they pass your house.

If you're honest with yourself, we've all seen it. These stories get plastered around the internet and passed around social media from Instagram to Facebook to Twitter. Here, they take on a more sinister momentum, encouraging racist white men and women to spew hateful rhetoric because they feel safe behind their keyboards and computer screens. These people have no problem using words like nigger, chink, spic; in fact, they wear their use like a badge of honor as they attempt to get a rise out of men and women of color. This is our norm. In the famed words of Donald Glover AKA Childish Gambino, "This is America."[35]

Growing up black means that you don't get the "birds and the bees" talk. Instead, you get the "how to act around police" talk.

"Hands at 2 and 10 at all times."

"No sudden movements."

"Always ask permission before reaching for your wallet."

"Yes, sir and no, sir, always."

"Be polite, no matter what."

When you think about it, this is something like a modern-day "shuck and jive," or speech intended to be sure the powerful white man doesn't come down on you too hard. Is it right that I had to have this talk with my parents while the children of Caucasian parents don't? Is it right that every time I see blue and red lights flashing behind me that my heart begins to race even though I've done absolutely nothing wrong? How about when I was skateboarding with friends after hours at school, and I was the only one put into handcuffs when the cops were called to kick us out? Is it right that when a white person screams in protest it's his or her American right but when a black person does it, he or she is viewed as a threat?

It goes even deeper than that. In high school and college, I had teachers that didn't believe I could do the work simply because I was black and therefore "harder to teach" because of my skin color. Now, growing up I was given every opportunity to succeed due to the fact that my parents worked hard to give me the best upbringing they could. But even with the supportive push forward I always had from them, I still faced difficulties because of something I had no control over: the color of my skin.

So, what do we do now?

How will this racist, 400 year-long chapter in America's history come to an end? How do we overcome the paradoxical perception of how power relationships between races should look in a country that has never been able to distribute power fairly or equally? These are the questions we should be asking.

When I was younger, I shared a thought process with one of my heroes:

"We declare our right on this earth to be a man, to be a human being, to be respected as a human being, to be given the rights of a human being in this society, on this earth, in this day, which we intend to bring into existence by any means necessary." - Malcom X[36]

"By any means necessary" rang true with me then and still does today. I will obtain my rights as a black man in America...by any means necessary. But this is where the lines start to become blurred; what exactly are "any means"? Does it mean being violent or protesting, or going to public forums and screaming into a microphone? It's difficult to know exactly what *should* be involved when going the peaceful route is so often confronted with violence in return. Whether it be from the police, or from bigoted citizens, or even by proxy from the silent masses who think that if something isn't affecting their lives then it's not important enough to stand up for.

What can I, Marc Hill, do to help? What can my voice do among the thousands chanting the same phrases year in and year out?

"I can't breathe!"

"Say their names!"

"We will not be silenced!"

Countless cries by countless members of the Black Lives Matter movement, worried for black men and women being brutalized and killed by other men and women with badges on a power trip. They are caught on tape, yet they are never convicted. What can we do? What can we do when the system is set up to reward the wicked and unjust while innocent men and women die at the hands of those who are supposed to protect us? Whether in this context or elsewhere, one of the most egregious **Paradoxes of Power** in the United States is the perception that if someone is in a position of power, whether it's a police officer, a politician, a CEO, a teacher, etc., that person must deserve that power and will surely wield it fairly. But how often is that actually the case? I may not be able to answer that question, but I strongly encourage you to ask it, at any time and in any place, because we *can* figure this out. We *can* do better.

We can start by educating others as to why we as a people are mad in the first place. Educate them, but not belittle them. If there is a willingness to learn about what has gotten us to this point in time in America, then there is hope. People need to understand that systemic racism exists, and that many families of color deal with it daily. They need to understand that countless lives have been affected by over-policing. They need to understand our TRUE history, and not the sugar-coated narrative our history books would have us believe. America's past is ugly and blood-soaked, too often at the expense of people who just wanted to understand us and coexist with us. From the near complete genocide of America's native peoples to the imprisonment of Japanese Americans during WWII, to the more recent border detention of migrants; from the Tulsa massacre to the countless backs of slaves torn to shreds by whips in the name of "building this great nation," we need to know every single aspect of our dark history so we can shine brighter as a nation and overcome this...*together as equals.*

From Ferguson to L.A., from New York to Minneapolis, the story is always the same...but it doesn't have to be. Let's try to be the change that James Baldwin, Malcom X, Martin Luther King Jr.,

Fred Hampton, and so many other revolutionaries wanted us to be. I think one of my favorite Black Panthers said it best:

"So we say - we always say in the Black Panther Party that they can do anything they want to do to us. We might not be back. I might be in jail, I might be anywhere. But when I leave, you'll remember I said, with the last word on my lips, that I am a revolutionary. And you're going to have to keep on saying that." - Fred Hampton[37]

I am a revolutionary.

Essay 4.3 – A Fictional Perspective

Sometimes it's useful to look at works of fiction to visualize the consequences of paradoxes. The following dialogue between protagonist, Steve, a white 30-something Texan, and Pauline, his French fiancé of the same age, are observations from the upcoming CE Hunt novel, *The Sommieres Sun*, to be published early 2021:

Sitting in my living room that afternoon surrounded by the ambiance of my creation: my books, my art, Indian pottery from New Mexico and my reproductions of Mayan and Aztec figures I had picked up mostly in Chihuahua, I poured myself a tall glass of red wine. I took a few deep breaths and just reflected on my time with Pauline and how much I missed her. I reflected particularly on a conversation I had with Pauline at the Bean Café in Presidio. She felt such at ease in Presidio. Maybe it was her Latin roots that put her at ease. France was an interesting combination of Latin and maybe Germanic culture. No surprise given the history of the country.

When I was in France, I felt it might be the ideal European culture. It at times evoked the precision and efficiency of Germany and the northern countries, but it also evoked at times the spontaneity, passion, art and freedom of the southern European countries. It certainly became more Latin as you went south. Pauline loved the potential of Mexico because it had the hope of being kind of the France of the western hemisphere in that it definitely evoked the artistry and freedom of southern Europe and added another element at times missing in Europe, a genuine warmth. Mexicans were among the kindest people that Pauline had ever met. She thought Mexico could be incredible, much better than the US, if only the Germans and Scandinavians would bring a bit more of their efficiency and precision to the nation.

Pauline felt that France had benefitted greatly from being a crossroads of Europe and being impacted by the north. She told me that the US could have had that potential if only the puritans would have kept their asses in England. She further opined that racism and slavery was a major impediment to the US achieving its full potential. She wasn't convinced that the US was going to be able to overcome that dark legacy.

At the Bean Café, we had the best conversation about United States policy towards Mexico. Pauline was convinced that we owed Mexico a great deal. She felt that the United States had violated Mexico's sovereignty so many times over the past couple of centuries. She had many good supporting arguments for that and had me convinced. She was amazed that Mexicans were still so warm to Americans. I explained to her that it was part of the beauty of the Mexican culture. It is who they are.

We discussed the cartel issue and she was astonished that the United States would spend endless sums of money to deal with the Taliban in Afghanistan but was so miserly in helping Mexico deal with the cartels. She practically demanded to know why putting down the Taliban was more important than helping a neighbor deal with the violence of cartels. She glared at me and said little girls in Mexican villages are important too! She said in France reports of what cartels do in Mexico are every bit as bad as what the Taliban is doing. Of course, who in the American government would look for insights from a newspaper in Europe?

I was shooting blanks when it came to countering her observations other than to point out that even though Mexico is a wonderful country with great people, corruption in their government has been a persistent challenge. That level of corruption probably helped create an opening for some of the criminal activities and certainly made reacting to it more difficult. She had me soul searching, wondering why having a peaceful neighbor wouldn't be a much higher priority for the United States. Part of me wondered if the United States should be more proactive in helping Mexico have stronger and more transparent civic institutions, or would Mexico be better off if we just left them alone and stopped providing a huge market for illegal drugs. There seemed no doubt to either one of us that our illicit markets for drugs in the US fueled much of the criminal activity.

She ended that conversation with an interesting observation, "Can you imagine the United States without Mexico? No workers to harvest the food you eat, no Mexican art and style, no Mexican food, no Mexican beer, no tequila and none of your precious margaritas, no tacos and enchiladas, no salsa. You'd just be a big, boring England with better, whiter teeth! Why can't people in the United States see that? The way some of your politicians talk about Mexicans! It is sickening."

5. Power In The Post-Pandemic Economy

A Tale of Two Paradoxes: Isolationism *and* Globalization

by Lawrence A. Kuznar[38]

E conomist Brian Arthur has written extensively on the subject he calls "complexity economics." Within this approach he describes three broad themes: modern economies are dynamic (i.e. they are constantly changing); encountering new and unique elements is not uncommon; and inductive reasoning is the key to understanding the rules and behaviors of our economies today. Arthur noted "(w)here equilibrium economics emphasizes order, determinacy, deduction, and stasis, complexity economics emphasizes contingency, indeterminacy, sense-making, and openness to change."[39] To paraphrase that statement, equilibrium economies are easier to understand and predict. Unfortunately, they are not an accurate representation of how things work "in the real world," leaving us to try and make sense of real-world economics, which defy predictability by their very nature.

Arthur's approach to understanding economies in a fast-moving and changing world also includes recognizing and projecting what a post-pandemic economy will look like. It provides an additional lens through which we might better understand **Paradoxes of Power** as they relate to rapidly changing, information-driven economies throughout a world responding to new opportunities and threats brought on by the pandemic.

In mid-April 2020, the journal <u>Foreign Affairs</u> published forecasts of the impact of the COVID-19 pandemic by nine leading economic scholars. Their predictions ranged from a future of greater connectivity and social justice to a less globalized economy to dire scenarios of economic collapse and political authoritarianism. Clearly, there is no consensus on what to expect. The forecasts posed serious questions to examine about our post-pandemic future and projected some fascinating directions in which our nation, our world and our interconnected economies might go.

Are we on the brink of global economic collapse? Will the pandemic be the watershed challenge to humanity that brings us all together? Do we face a future that pits factions against one another within countries and countries against one another as they seek to protect their identities, supply lines, and borders? How can the nation's most brilliant economists be so diametrically opposed? Examining history gives us substantial clues about what to expect during and after this pandemic, and where **Paradoxes of Power** between nations and within nations are more likely to occur as a result.

There have been many plagues and epidemics throughout history, but the 1918-1919 H1N1 Influenza pandemic is a good starting point to understand what we face in 2020, as it produced the most data concerning its effects on the U.S. and the global economy in relatively modern times.[40] Elizabeth Brainerd and Mark Siegler (2003) of the Centre for Economic Policy Research conducted a detailed study of the effects of the H1N1 pandemic on per capita GDP in the United States, in which they controlled for key factors such as education, labor supply, climate, and per capita influenza deaths.

Brainerd and Siegler write that the 1918 pandemic killed at least 40 million people world-wide and at least 550,000 Americans, which amounted to 0.66% of the U.S. population. One notable feature of H1N1 was its random impacts across the socioeconomic spectrum and geography. The pandemic seemed to impact the poor and wealthy alike; deaths were concentrated in states that had little in common, such as Pennsylvania, Kansas, and Montana, while many states experienced much less trauma.

Ironically, the pandemic preceded "The Roaring 20s," which was a time of unprecedented economic growth for the U.S. and the world, with most workers experiencing an increased standard of living. The specific economic effect of the pandemic was a decreased supply of labor, which forced firms to increase wages. The labor supply was reduced in the short run because of a peculiarity of the influenza; the disease disproportionately attacked the prime labor force (ages 15-44 at that time), along with the very young and very old. The labor supply was also reduced in the long run due to a sharp decrease (about 10%) in life expectancy during the pandemic and decreased fertility afterward.

A couple of factors confounded the pandemic's influence. The end of WWI was followed by a period of recovery as Europe and North America transitioned to peace-time economies, as is typical after major conflicts. This is a well-known phenomenon and constitutes a first-order effect of war—regrowth. However, the economic boom unexpectedly created new opportunities in politics (women's suffrage), education, and employment for women. These newfound opportunities motivated women to prioritize careers over having children, further reducing the size of the labor force.

These compounded, interactive effects are more than ironic, in fact. They also reflect an emergence, or unexpected result, as Carl Hunt described in Chapter 1 and in Appendix B. No government or business intended these outcomes, and they were themselves products of unforeseen exchanges between the economic and political structures, as is typical of a complex system that demonstrates an emergence.[41] The irony lies in that the pandemic and WWI were tragedies for human life, but a windfall for the global economic system and the rise of women's rights. The end of WWI also produced effects that demonstrated power shifts that were paradoxical indeed.

The 1920s might have been "roaring" but they also sent the US and the world into the tailspin of the Great Depression and an even greater global conflict in WWII and the subsequent Cold War. The amount of blood and treasure many nations expended during these times produced post-war economies we would never have projected at the dawn of the 20th Century. Truly an example of emergence at work! If Carl Hunt's thesis about **Paradoxes of Power** also being emergences is correct, this result also suggests such a paradox as it reflects outcomes that could not have been deduced by examining the objectives of the participants during their post-war planning and recovery period.

So, let's not cast off our masks and head to the beach party just yet. We are not out of the woods in 2020, just as we were not in the 1920s, because pandemics have effects beyond the economic. Often, the shock of a catastrophe is not the quandary; our reaction to the shock is the problem. This is where emergence is truly in effect and paradoxes thrive. We'll focus on more of the power relationship shifts and the true **Paradoxes of Power** next.

For instance, colleague Ian Lustick of the University of Pennsylvania made a compelling argument that one of the biggest tragedies for the U.S. of the 9-11 terrorist attacks was not only the terrible loss of the lives of nearly 3000 Americans. Rather it was also the country's reaction, which cost more than 3000 U.S. service members' lives, trillions of dollars, and hundreds of thousands of civilian lives abroad. U.S. invasions destabilized Afghanistan and especially Iraq and the Middle East, and we continue to see the consequences of these actions today (Lustick, 2006). In a similar way, reactions to the 1918 pandemic had a vastly greater global impact than the 50 million lost lives and any possible short-term economic decline. None were desired or expected by world leaders, and these reactions spun out of control because of a lack of recognition, foresight and leadership.

Brainerd and Siegler show us that the economic impacts of the 1918 pandemic appear to have been minimal, and actually beneficial for the nation as a whole, although those benefits were not shared equally. Laura Spinney's book, *Pale Rider* (2017) describes many of the unanticipated 2nd and 3rd order effects and failures of leadership imposing additional catastrophic effects on the world. In the U.S., Black Americans were impacted more severely by the virus, and working-class families that lost a male bread-winner effectively lost their livelihoods and endured great poverty. In Germany, veteran enlisted men and laborers did not share equally in the post-war boom, and were recruited by a certain small, radical group that leaders of the time largely dismissed and ridiculed for its outlandish ideas, as did economic and social power wielders.[42]

German cities that experienced high per capita flu deaths in 1918 wound up spending less on investments that could support jobs and benefit the young, which fueled the discontent of minorities and immigrants (Bickle, 2020). If you currently live in the United States, this scenario may sound eerily familiar. The post-war economic boom also fueled rampant economic speculation world-wide, left unchecked because of greed, which culminated in the stock market crash of 1929 that plunged the world into an economic depression. This was a cascade of events that led to one paradoxical outcome after another. The leaders of the 1920s neither wanted the rise of Nazi extremism nor a global economic collapse. But these unanticipated minor currents grew unchecked into waves of global catastrophe; all that was needed was a spark to accelerate them. The Great Depression *was* that spark, and another **Paradox of Power** manifested as events unfolded in ways no single "member of the group" desired. You could almost say the whole world was "on the bus to Abilene" as Carl and Joshua detailed in Chapter 1.

In Germany, the Great Depression provided the obscure National Socialist Party with a golden opportunity. Now legions of working-class Germans were disoriented and discontented with their own government, and the formerly reviled losers from WWI and the pandemic (the Nazis) became viewed as many Germans' saviors (Bickle, 2020; Spinney, 2017). In the U.S., preoccupation with the Great Depression reinforced isolationist policies that prevented it and its allies from confronting the growing German threat (Spinney, 2017). The result: WWII and 85 million dead, a terrifying 3% of the world's population. None except the most devout Nazi believers wanted that, and even they couldn't understand the potential consequences of starting a war as all-encompassing as WWII.

The 1918 pandemic cannot be solely blamed for the social discontents that resulted in WWII, but it was a factor on a complex web of events, not unlike the emergence of economies such as those Brian Arthur discusses in complexity economics. Fortunately, in recent history, pandemics do not seem to cause these kinds of major change. They do, however, appear to accelerate ongoing trends and to enable unexpectedly powerful forces that likely would never have manifested if governments had acted quickly once the pandemic effects began to appear. This is much like what we saw in the US in the first half of 2020; the delays and various federal and state missteps resulted in the emergence of a negative force on our population and economies. This is one **Paradox of Power** we could have seen coming and mitigated before it grew out of control.

But if we can understand the differences between 1918 and 2020, all is not lost! A comparison of 1918's H1N1 and the COVID-19 pandemic of today can provide insights into what is more or less likely to occur in the future. Each comparison point is explained below.

Table 1. Comparison of 1918 H1N1 Pandemic and 2020 COVID-19 Pandemic

1918 H1N1 Influenza Pandemic	2020 COVID-19 Pandemic
Highly contagious and virulent	Same
U.S. deaths 0.07% per capita	U.S. deaths 0.007% per capita
Driven by international travel	Same
Variable impacts in U.S. geographically	Same
Followed by an economic boom	????
Increased inequality and resentment	Same
Fueled nationalism & authoritarianism	Same
Followed destructive global war	No major destructive global war (as of this writing)
Infected and killed the most economically productive members of society	Infected and killed least economically productive members of society
Industrial/agrarian economy	Information/service economy

Will the same emergent results produce a modern post-pandemic economy for the US and the rest of the world? Will the post-pandemic world experience an economic boom equivalent to the post 1918 pandemic? That is hard to determine at this point, although predictions of economic collapse are probably premature for several reasons. First, COVID-19 infects and kills the elderly disproportionately (> age 65 consistently accounting for between 70 – 88 % of deaths), and is for the most part (although not entirely) less devastating to young adults and children (New York City Health, 2020; Novel Coronavirus Pneumonia Emergency Response Epidemiology Team, 2020; White & Nafilyan, 2020). Therefore, COVID-19 is taking out, statistically speaking, the least economically productive members of society and leaving the most productive and future productive members alone. Post-pandemic economies from a large-scale view may simply be back to business as usual.

Based on what we have seen so far, no significant labor shortages or major demographic shifts should occur. Once the pandemic runs its course or we implement a vaccine, the world can get "back to business" and the demands for goods and services (and the labor to produce them) will resume in earnest.[43] On the other hand, the current situation lacks the previous global devastation of a world war, so we may not experience an economic boom, either. Longer term, some unanticipated second-order economic impacts that may have a more insidious effect are described below.

With respect to similarities, both viruses are highly contagious. The death rate from the 1918 H1N1 was 2.5%, which compares to the relatively consistent 3% death rate COVID-19 is seeing globally. Both have highly variable impacts nationwide. The 1918 H1N1 affected some states severely such as Pennsylvania and Kansas, but other states were barely touched. The New York City metropolitan area was initially a hotspot for COVID-19, and although the virus has spread to nearly all counties in the U.S., its impact is much lower (1/20th the death rate in most counties compared to the New York metropolitan region) and highly variable. This is based on an on-going research project that I have personally conducted to prepare for this essay and other projects. As mentioned, working class families that lost a breadwinner and Black American families were most impacted, both biologically and economically, by the 1918 H1N1. The same has been true for COVID-19; Black Americans have borne the brunt of the effects of the death rates and working class families in manufacturing and service sectors have been economically devastated. Left unchecked, inequality will likely increase, providing opportunities for divisive politicians to exploit race and class resentment and increase the threat of violence as a result.[44]

The variable experience with the virus has fueled confusion and division. New Yorkers who see mass graves in Central Park are confronted with a dramatic reminder that the pandemic is here and is undeniably deadly. In contrast, lower death rates than originally in the northeast (so far) and extremely variable encounters in the American Heartland have given doubters license to dismiss it as "just the flu" or worse, a liberal hoax designed to unseat a president.

The same turn towards nationalism and authoritarianism, previously witnessed in Germany between the world wars, is accompanying the COVID-19 pandemic in many nations worldwide: China, Russia, Hungary, Great Britain, France, Germany, Poland, and even the US, to name a few. Just as with the 1918 pandemic, these are social, economic, and political trends that pre-dated the pandemic; COVID-19 has simply accelerated them. In the U.S., early refusal by the Center for Disease Control to commit to a stance on masks fueled popular skepticism about science and expertise, and turned the virus into a political sideshow. The current President's dismissal of the pandemic and refusal to lead by example has only furthered the cause for those who subscribe to it and has rationalized extreme behavior; Americans have actually killed one another over wearing masks. What will be next?

I see here a tale of two paradoxes, one short-term with potential long-term consequences, and the other a long-term contradiction of all the rhetoric and concern over economic isolation. In the short-term, politicians will embrace the opportunity to stoke nationalistic and isolationist policies in order to garner more autocratic control over their nations on behalf of themselves and their constituencies (Kahl & Berengaut, 2020)—they will have, by definition, ceased to work on behalf of the collective whole. This is paradox one, which may lead to a less stable and likely less "free" world, and one in which governments could become frighteningly more reminiscent of dictatorships than democracies.

However, an opposite trend could contradict this paradox. Countries may want to protect supply lines and focus economies within their borders. The truth is that producers of goods and services want cheap labor and supplies, and consumers want cheap goods and services. The very people that support nationalistic policies will demand cheap goods on the market and the profit seekers will look for cheap labor and new markets to sell their goods; globalization will be far from dead. Just as it thrived after 1918, it will most likely thrive after 2020. This is paradox two. If this pandemic was a flood, wielders and yielders of power are most likely going to rebuild on the same flood plain. The world is most likely to become a contradiction of nationalist rhetoric and xenophobia that will be more economically interconnected and interdependent than ever. Which means that the next major shock will ripple through all nations and the disruption will be felt by all again. Everyone will seem surprised, although there will be nothing surprising about it. This is a paradox cycle we should be looking to break… now, while we recognize it early!

No one planned this pandemic, and no rational person would want it to continue. It is the product of a complex system that few take the time to understand, fewer yet have the courage to confront, and too many think they can control simplistically. Take heart, there is hope, but only if we work to avoid the paradoxes outlined above. The generation that currently holds power has arguably failed and continues down a path from which there eventually may be no return. The generations which are preparing to "take the reins" must learn from this failure, and we all must work together to see that we don't continue to make the same mistakes.

Chapter 1's section on mitigation and avoidance and the essays in Chapters 7 and 8 attempt to provide some guidelines for taking control now and as Chapter 1 prescribes: staying off "The Bus to Abilene."

References

Bickle, K. (2020). *Pandemics Change Cities: Municipal Spending and Voter Extremism in Germany, 1918-1933*. Federal Reserve Bank of New York Staff Report No. 921. New York.

Brainerd, E., & Siegler, M. V. (2003). *The Economic Effects of the 1918 Influenza Epidemic*. CEPR Discussion Paper No. 3791. Centre for Economic Policy Research, London.

Brinton, C. (1964). *The Anatomy of Revolution, Revised and Expanded Edition*. New York: Vintage Books.

Burke, K. (1974). The Rhetoric of Hitler's "Battle". In K. Burke (Ed.), *The Philosophy of Literary Form: Studies in Symbolic Action, Third Edition* (pp. 191-220). Berkeley, California: University of California Press.

Daly, M. (2016). *Killing the Competition: Economic Inequality and Homicide*. New York: Transaction Publishers.

Kahl, C. H., & Berengaut, A. (2020). Aftershocks: The Coronavirus Pandemic and the New World Disorder. Retrieved from https://warontherocks.com/2020/04/aftershocks-the-coronavirus-pandemic-and-the-new-world-disorder/

Kuznar, L. A. (2007). Rationality Wars and the War on Terror: Explaining Terrorism and Social Unrest. *American An-*

thropologist, 109(2), 318-329.

Lustick, I. S. (2006). *Trapped in the War on Terror*. Philadelphia: University of Pennsylvania Press.

New York City Health. (2020). *Coronavirus disease 2019 (COVID-19) Daily Data Summary*. New York City.

Novel Coronavirus Pneumonia Emergency Response Epidemiology Team. (2020). The Epidemiological Characteristics of an Outbreak of 2019 Novel Coronavirus Diseases (COVID-19) — China, 2020. *China CDC Weekly, 2*(8), 113-122. Retrieved from http://weekly.chinacdc.cn/en/article/id/e53946e2-c6c4-41e9-9a9b-fea8db1a8f51

Orwell, G. (1968). Review of *Mein Kampf* by Adolf Hitler. In S. O. I. Angus (Ed.), *The Collected Essays, Journalism and Letters of George Orwell, Volume 2,* . New York: Harcourt Brace Jovanovich.

Spinney, L. (2017). *Pale Rider: The Spanish Flu of 1918 and How It Changed the World*. London: Cape.

White, C., & Nafilyan, V. (2020). *Coronavirus-related deaths by ethnic group, England and Wales methodology*. London, Office for National Statistics.

6. Human Power Versus Nature's Power

by C. E. Hunt & Carl W. Hunt

Paradoxes of Power come in many shapes and contexts. The most challenging to overcome are the ones you don't even realize exist because you're too distracted achieving what feels like significant success. When some 7.8 billion people are sharing to varying degrees in the success from which you benefit, it's even more difficult to realize the extent of the paradox that is affecting you. You can't see the proverbial forest for the trees. That's what has been happening since the advent of the Industrial Age. This "success" presents us with the most challenging paradox we've ever faced.

One way to visualize what's happened in our world in the last century and a half is to consider our circumstances as a story of what could be a future scenario.

Imagine our planet and the thin fragile patina of biosphere on its surface as a "closed system," perhaps like a large spaceship. As a closed system, other than the energy we get from the sun, all our sustenance, such as food, water and oxygen, comes from the interior of our "spaceship." We started out with what seemed like unlimited resources, but as we traveled through space and time, we could begin to see our storehouse dwindling. There's nothing to worry about for a long time, right? There'll be plenty of time to fix that, won't there?

For whatever reason, in perhaps the ultimate paradox of power, we also imagine that we are in charge of our spaceship and its "environmental control system" is functioning perfectly. We act as though the chemical, physical and biological realities of our spaceship-planet have no power to which we must yield or at least respect, because everything seems to work acceptably. We can exploit it to our hearts' content and be as creative and productive as we like. Speaking of being creative, each new human added to the crew of our spaceship stretches our finite resources even more, but there's plenty of time to fix that, too... right?

Imagine a spaceship crew that because of these misconceptions continues to burn fuel on their spaceship that gradually is heating the inside of the spaceship even though they know at some point the excess heat will set in motion many changes that make the interior uninhabitable. Or perhaps the crew engages in behaviors that have no respect for other crew members (humans and non-humans). It's no big deal, of course, because we're making good livings and building our societies, cities and businesses at as fast a pace as possible because that's how we make money and live better. We may have to change someday, but there's still plenty of time, right?

Imagine conversations between the crew and an imaginary "Mission Control" that "oversees" our journey. Some call this control system God, some call it Mother Nature, some don't even think about it at all. Such a dialogue might go like this:[45]

"Earthship Crew Number One, this is Mission Control. We note the temperature on your spacecraft is increasing at an unsustainable pace. Major degradation to your interior, likely involving the death of many or all crew members is almost certain before the end of your voyage. Over."

"Mission Control, our comfort is paramount. We are not willing to sacrifice yet. We don't see why we should change anything at this time. Besides, some of the crew in other parts of the ship will continue burning the fuel inside the craft as they please, whether or not we change. Over."

"Crew One, 98% of our readings indicate massive heating will result in a premature termination of voyage. It will be grim. Over."

"Mission Control, we are banking on the 2% of readings suggesting the potential of greater resilience. We think your science is wrong and doing what we please is more important. We are unwilling to change our behavior. Over."

"Crew One, are you comfortable betting the lives of your children and the non-humans on board on the 2% chance? Over."

"Affirmative. Our immediate comfort and way of life are paramount. Over"

Or perhaps this conversation:

"Mission control, the members of Crew One want more space so we are going to occupy zones 23 and 24 of the spacecraft. Over"

"Crew One, that's a problem. Zone 23 is for non-human members of the crew. Zone 24 is for the lower income crew members. Over."

"Mission Control, no problem. The inhabitants of both zones will be relocated to Zone 100. Over.

"Crew One, Zone 100 is a marginal habitat. Survival questionable. Over."

"Mission Control, we are prepared to risk it. Over."

"Crew One, the lower income members of the crew as well as the non-human members of your crew will likely become extinct. They are the ones at risk, not you. Over."

"Mission Control. We need the space. Our comfort is important too. Over."

Wow. Those conversations could never happen, could they? Some readers will suggest this is hyperbolic, but we would contend it really isn't that farfetched if you come to see our planet as a closed system as far as our survival is concerned. Since we don't really have spaceships that can transport us off our home planet yet, it's not that hyperbolic to visualize our environment like that at all. It is paradoxical but not exaggerated.

This **Paradox of Power**, where we perceive the needs of the planet that supplies all of our water, food and oxygen as well as the only habitat we have, as only an afterthought, if at all, is in many respects the ultimate paradox. Here's the thing: we just *think* we know how nature will react to our failure to yield or at least share power with her. Let us describe a theory to help better understand that reality. It has a curious name, but it is powerful once you grasp it. It is called the "The Adjacent Possible." We'll share a little more background first though.

Three years ago, Dr. Stuart A. Kauffman, began to deeply research and document the circumstances surrounding our long sought-after national and global economies.[46] Kauffman has laid bare how our increasingly interconnected economies are also damaging our future as both the human species and indeed all life on earth. The best human thinking, planning and engineering in our history is leading to one of the worst possible outcomes, a result we couldn't start to imagine at the beginning of an economic expansion fueled since at least the start of the Industrial Age.

One could quote Charles Dickens from 1859 in *A Tale of Two Cities*: "It was the best of times, it was the worst of times, it was the age of wisdom, it was the age of foolishness...." Dickens' inspired writing reflects paradox and struggle, and in the context of economic expansion, our struggle against nature is still alive today. The power struggles to which we rarely pay attention relative to the interactions of mankind and nature are not only paradoxes, they're life threatening.

The year is now 2020. Our $100 trillion-plus global economy is growing around 3-4% a year and lifting millions from poverty.[47] It links our globe in trade and provides the means by which we earn our livings. This economy is highly interactive and richly complex. While it is certain COVID-19 is signifi- cantly affecting our national and global economies at the time of writing this essay, it's nonetheless clear that we are liv- ing with the consequences of decades of loosely constrained growth. This same growing global economy has also been driv- ing climate change and setting the stage for mass extinction events. These same richly complex interactions between man and nature cloak what has been happening over the past two centuries. It was the "business as usual" path that dominated, or so we mistakenly thought...another paradox.

Today, Dickens' "best of times" is our unfettered growth in the global market and technological development; the "worst of times" is the equally unrestrained and imminent destruction of so many species and the environment in which we live. The mu- tual interactions of these best and worst times added a level of obscurity that have until recently confounded the best think- ing and human leadership in both science and policymaking.

This led us to recall the notion of "Spaceship Earth" dating back to at least the mid-1960s when R. Buckminster Fuller intro- duced the term. He created the idea "to enable all of humanity to live with freedom, comfort and dignity, without negatively impacting the earth's ecosystems or regenerative ability." He advised that we "learn to command this Spaceship to avert glo- bal crisis and catastrophe and ensure the long-term success of humanity," [48] something which we don't seem to have taken to heart yet. The metaphor is appropriate in any event.

For this reason, we consider the earth a largely closed system, even though it is obviously still impacted by our sun and other extraterrestrial objects. As far as life-sustaining elements, what we have here is all we have. Once it's gone, it's gone. Thus, it's easy to think of the earth as a spaceship with extremely limited resources we are consuming quickly. In short, we are making our spaceship gradually inhospitable to all living creatures, in- cluding humans. Very likely, in the not-too-distant future, even the more environmentally conscientious among us may be seen with the same derision that many of us now hold for poachers of endangered species.

NY Times columnist Thomas Friedman notes we as the human race have been steadily removing all the buffers that nature and even prior generations of mankind have put into place, including national and international regulations, to chase "short-term efficiency and growth." In so doing, we've made the world extremely brittle and easier to damage through events such as the COVID-19 pandemic. And, since there's "no immunity to greed," as Friedman writes, there doesn't appear to be anything on the horizon short of nature's intervention (e.g., a pandemic or global climate change) to slow us down.[49]

The UN Intergovernmental Science-Policy Platform on Biodiversity and Ecosystem Services Report of 6 May 2019 provided two sobering observations: 1.) "The average abundance of native species in most major land-based habitats has fallen by at least 20%, mostly since 1900," and around one-million species are threatened with extinction by 2050; and 2.) "More than a third of the world's land surface and nearly 75% of freshwater resources are now devoted to crop or livestock production."[50]

In recent science presentations, Stuart Kauffman often quotes from the UN reports of 2019 because it's so dramatic and so impeccably sourced. If you're human, it should also be frightening how much Mother Nature is pushing back against our attempts to claim dominion over her, also documented in the UN report. As Kauffman notes in his presentations, we are of the world, not above the world, and thus this is a fight we cannot win. It's a paradox we will not overcome without change on our part.

Our current geological era, often dubbed the Anthropocene, roughly describes the earth under the influence of humanity, including the changes to the environment that human civilization has experienced, if not caused.[51] All these exchanges between humans and nature highlight the pitting of interests and power of humans against the disinterested power of nature. At the current rate, the malfunction of the environmental control system of our spaceship will lead to a premature ending of our collective mission.

Theory of the Adjacent Possible

Kauffman, now 80, a former Marshall Scholar and past MacArthur Fellow, as well as a medical doctor and theoretical biologist, has made understanding the futility of these power struggles between man and nature his recent life's work. He's recently augmented his thinking in a concept called the "Theory of the Adjacent Possible," or TAP. The ideas composing TAP come from early 2002 research Kauffman did when he called it simply "The Adjacent Possible."

"The Adjacent Possible is what can arise next out of what exists now. For example, once the iPhone exists, smartphone apps to run on those iPhones are in the adjacent possible and come to exist," but they couldn't have existed before, Kauffman explains. "We cannot say what is in the adjacent possible ahead of time. This is shown by my "Screwdriver argument." We cannot pre-state in a list all the uses of a screwdriver; novelty and innovation in the use of a screwdriver just keep unfolding as the screwdriver is used. This is fundamental to innovation in both the evolution of the biosphere and econosphere."[52]

The thinking about the adjacent possible is fundamental to understanding where we as a species have taken our global economy and the natural environment in which we all live. It has to do with a phenomenon called coevolution. Things don't typically evolve without a stimulus or prodding from something else. Two forces or objects come together and exert some influence on each other, and both change or evolve in a coupling that's related to their interactions: the two things coevolve. Something new emerges, emergence being another term that Kauffman and other theorists known as complexity scientists use in the context of the results of a coevolution.[53]

The adjacent possible spins out the coevolved concept, object, thing or whatever is the result of the interactions of the concepts, objects or things that existed before. Things need some "next" environment to emerge into something new, and that environment for emergent novelty is the adjacent possible. It's just not as predictable as we'd like, if at all, because we simply can't pre-state the possibilities. That's why life, innovation and even power paradoxes are complex and understanding them is so difficult.[54]

Is it possible to demonstrate this in a mathematical or formulaic way to help visualize what's happening in the technologically-driven econosphere, as Kauffman calls it? He and his codevelopers of TAP, Wim Hordijk, Mike Steel and Roger Koppl, say that there is.[55] The TAP process, in equation form, looks like this:

$$M_{t+1} = M_t + \sum_{i=1}^{M_t} \alpha_i \binom{M_t}{i}$$

At first, Kauffman called this the "napkin model" according to Hordijk, since he initially wrote it on a dinner napkin at the Santa Fe Bar and Grill in 2017. "The concept is simpler that it might look. M_t is the number of 'goods' or 'tools' in an economy at time t. Say M_t is 40. M_t+1 is the number of goods in the economy in the next period, say a year. All the equation says is that the number of goods in the next period is the number of goods present now, M_t, plus all the new goods that can be made by trying to make something useful from any one among the 40, or pairs of things among the 40, or triplets among the 40, and so on," Kauffman explained.

This TAP process is just the creative exploration of what is possible next, the *adjacent possible*, given what is *actual* now. This formula accommodates the reality of combinatorial growth over time, which is observed in what's known as the "hockey stick" curve. The growth in the number of tools increases glacially for a very long time and then suddenly explodes upward in a hockey-stick-like curve. This is observable in the real world according to Kauffman and his colleagues.

An example of this hockey-stick curve and explosive growth shows up in an examination of Global GDP over the last 2000 years.[56] As the chart below shows, the growth begins around 1700, modestly rising around the period of 1820 to 1870, and then begins to sky-rocket from 1900 to 1950 when it becomes almost vertical growth each year from that point. According to "Our World in Data" sources, we've gone from a global GDP of around $643 billion in 1700 to well over $100 trillion in just over 300 years (as of 2017).

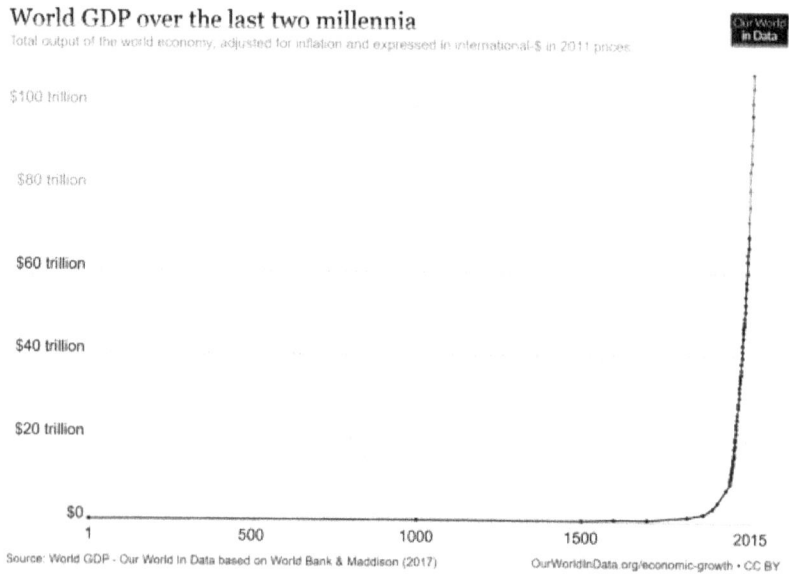

Kauffman's theory captures this growth dynamic in terms of goods and services. As Kauffman describes, "TAP hopes to explain glacial growth in the number of goods and GDP for hundreds of thousands of years, then the explosion upward in the last few centuries. We have gone from perhaps a thousand goods

5,000 years ago to billions today. The same theory accounts for the glacial, then explosive growth of differentiation of goods into simple and increasingly complex types of goods and services.

"20,000 years ago, Cro-Magnon had perhaps 200 simple tools ranging from arrow heads to the spear thrower. Now we humans have billions ranging from needles to satellites and the Space Station. This cumulative innovation is the major driver of economic growth. We essentially recombine whatever we have and accumulate what works. TAP is the first mathematical theory of this process of cumulative cultural evolution," Kauffman concludes.

So, what's the issue? Humans are wonderfully creative and use the tools and goods they've previously created to build new capabilities. That's just smart innovation, right?

As Princeton University Ecology and Evolutionary Biology Professor Simon Levin points out, the innovations humans "introduce to solve local or even national-level problems create unintended negative global consequences." He describes examples such as coal-fired electricity plants; every state or nation provides power to a community or region and produces emissions that cumulatively pollute the rest of the world. When we think about GDP growth that lifts entire populations out of poverty, we also need to consider the following that demonstrate similar growth curves: energy production; logging; mining of the materials needed to construct these goods and fuel power plants; lands developed to provide animal and vegetable foods; waterway uses for drinking and unfortunately, waste products; and anything else that supports GDP growth.

All of this has worked out okay for humans so far, but it's starting to look like it may not be so good for many of the other species on our earth. The major issue for us is that if one species dies out, the effects may not be felt for decades or centuries, if at all. However, if a million species become extinct in such a short time, we have no way of projecting how it will affect humanity and our biosphere. It may be too late for us to "fix" anything at that point; even human power could be rendered useless in that situation. That may be the ultimate paradox in human history!

Wim Hordijk may sum it up best. "In my view, one of the main problems is that in our increasingly urbanized and modernized society, humanity seems to have lost its connection with the natural world. However, not only are we part of this natural world, we very much depend on it," he wrote. Hordijk's and Kauffman's perspectives are the same, and the partnership between nature and man requires our attention, immediately and always.

Most of the popular press talks about climate change and the likely effects it will have for people who live along the coast or in areas that are experiencing hotter and dryer than normal weather. These changes clearly disturb human life and our economies with floods and fires and other changes we may not have normally experienced in our lifetimes. We don't yet know the relationships of these changes to the COVID-19 pandemic, but there is likely to be an observable chain of events coming out of a review of our experiences in coming years.

Thomas Friedman also writes about the idea of the disturbances we cause with "...Mother Nature. She is not a contestant on 'The Apprentice.' She is just chemistry, biology and physics. We're the contestants on her show. We don't get to fire her. She gets to fire us. She throws viruses, hurricanes, floods, droughts, heat waves and pandemics at us to sort out who's the fittest. And the ones who survive have one thing, and one thing only, in common: They are the most adaptive at generating the chemistry, biology and physics needed to meet the challenge. That's all that matters. All those who can't, get fired, or rather, are returned to the manufacturer."[57]

If we accept Kauffman's observations that humans are part of nature, however, and not above it, we can start to appreciate that these changes impact all life everywhere. Thanks to Stuart Kauffman and other thought leaders with whom he's worked and influenced, we now have even more indicators, such as TAP, to substantiate what's happening in our world as the 2020s begin. We can now observe in objective models and from our own empirical observations such as those reflected in the UN reports, the results and likely outcomes of human "success" in technology and economy building. Before, it was hard to see all these factors working together and what their interactions might yield.

Our main challenge has been that we simply didn't understand the complexities that are inherent in life and our environment, and both are changing...coevolving. We didn't have enough insights about the biosphere to appreciate what happens when we lose species and the cascade of effects that such losses unleash. Species extinction, particularly at the scale about which Kauffman and his colleagues are warning us, and as verified by recent UN studies, informs us of the impending dangers. We can now begin to see the overwhelmingly complex issues that tended to drive us towards uncertainty and inaction. This must change. People must exercise responsible leadership.

Humans and the power they collectively wield represent the only real chance of what we might call "biosphere leadership" on behalf of all our fellow species, and we've been failing miserably. We've chosen to make as much money, create as much technology and energy as possible, and generally opt for our own conveniences and luxury.

If we don't take leadership responsibility and resolve the power paradoxes between man and nature, we avoid these duties without excuse. One of the first obligations leaders in all fields are taught is the idea behind stewardship and resource allocation. We take care of our people and they take care of us as leaders. We responsibly manage our scarce and precious resources to succeed and those resources work to the benefit of all…that's good leadership and the way to avoid a **Paradox of Power**.

In summary, Kauffman's Theory of the Adjacent Possible (TAP) begins to elegantly show how our human role in the world has played out and how practically inevitable it was that we harmed our larger world while we individually chased the promise of great success. Studying TAP, it's hard to see how it could have been any different given we understood so little about the complexity of the biosphere up to this point, and ultimately shirked leadership responsibilities for actions to protect our world.

The good news is that there's no need for our mission as a species to "end prematurely" if we can reassess and correct the paradox in our relationship with nature. We, as the crew of our spaceship, can have a robust future if we can learn to yield to Mother Nature's power when needed to ensure the sustainability of our lives as a species.

In a proper power relationship with Mother Nature, she will take care of us and continue to deliver the many free goods to both the human and non-human crews of our spaceship that are so important to us all: clean water, clean air, calories, recreation, spiritual renewal, raw ingredients for technology and all the staples of life.

We can thus be hopeful that once we address our **Paradox of Power** with nature, the conversation would go more like…

"Crew One, this is Mission Control. We note the temperature on your spacecraft is increasing at an unsustainable pace. Major degradation to your interior, likely involving the death of many or all crew members, almost certain before the end of your voyage. Over."

"Copy that Mission Control. Appropriate adjustments under way. We're taking care of it now."

7. Government, Politics And Education

by Carl W. Hunt and Lawrence A. Kuznar

This chapter of **Paradoxes of Power** is simultaneously the easiest and most challenging essay we've written for this book. Because of our combined 75+ years of government and academic service, we have a thorough understanding of both systems and can discuss them with relative ease. On the other hand, this body of experience and everything we have gained from it generates some level of bias that we must overcome to objectively critique these organizations. In the end, we concluded that we had to follow our nation's Founders' principles; we acknowledged that the United States of America is still very much an experiment and work in progress, and one that demands constant review and constructive criticism. Thus, this chapter may approach our subjects a bit more academically...no apologies, just stating our methodology up front as good academic approaches should.

Earnest students of our United States Constitution realize that even its Framers understood the difficulties of building a nation on the principles they held up—freedom balanced by security and opportunity balanced by fairness. All of this was envisioned to be tempered by equal treatment under the law. The beauty of the work the Framers did was in creating a Constitution in which these apparent competing factors and contradictions could be resolved without paradox and the new United States of America could take its place as a new kind of nation in world history. The Framers knew it would not be easy. When Benjamin Franklin was asked whether our Constitution granted us a republic, he famously quipped, "A republic, if you can keep it."

Moreover, the Framers also knew they couldn't get it right the first time, and they included a system for correction and amendment in the form of Article V. The authors of our Constitution including its original defenders, Hamilton, Madison, and Jay (collectively known as Publius), understood the importance of adapting to changing times and shifting public perspectives, even if they had no way of predicting what those would look like in the future. It is this original willingness to adjust to change that we embrace in the writing of this essay.[58]

This essay and the next, Chapter 8 on Religion and Justice, look at some of the most impacting **Paradoxes of Power** that have occurred in the last 50 years or so, since around the period Richard Nixon served as our nation's 37th President.[59] We will not closely examine the presidencies of our leaders since that time, but rather look at the trends in the exercise of power that took place during these last five decades. Over the course of these years, there have been significant events that have shaped our nation through today, going into the elections of 2020. Some of the important and more significant events of this period have greatly divided our nation and created uncertainty as to how our future as the United States of America will unfold over the next 50 years. Several events offer great promise and hope, while some paint a dark cloud over the future of our nation, and perhaps humanity.

If you've followed the influence of power paradoxes in our nation through the previous essays, you realize that our nation's power relationship issues aren't restricted to human organizational and political malfunctions. There are a variety of factors involved in landing us where we are today. Some of these factors include a quest to dominate political and government relationships, failure of education, misapplication of religious principles, failure to appreciate our role in nature, and a general loss of appreciation and respect for those on the "other side" of the issues we personally embrace. Each of these influences interact and serve to strengthen resolve to maintain one's own stand on the concerns that affect our nation the most, even to the point of intransigence.[60] The remainder of this chapter and the next chapter address the pieces that make up these interactions.[61]

We talked quite a bit about the clash of human power and nature's power in Chapter 6, so we won't repeat that here other than to say what we learned from thinkers like Stuart Kauffman and Thomas Friedman can extend to creating a greater appreciation for the other areas, as well. For example, thinking about our relationship with people who represent the "other" side of the political spectrum can produce ways we achieve respect and collaboration for beliefs over which we cannot exercise control. Just as we can't force nature to accept all our carbon emissions, we also cannot force Democrats to think like Republicans. However, we could accommodate each other and find ways to coexist so that each side can benefit...we might encourage Democrats and Republicans to think first like Americans before they cling to party preferences. If we look for win-win scenarios we just might find them, as we have in the past. In the case of nature, that also means that many other species beside us benefit...win-win-win.

Let's look at this in another way. This is a widely diverse and even peaceful nation if "viewed from space."[62] A visitor from another planet could look at the US from a distance and we would appear to embrace perspectives of all political and religious persuasions—in spite of protest marches that occasionally get out of hand, there are no military battles being fought across our lands. If they had read our founding documents, our visitor from another world would likely conclude the US is a cohesive and united nation, given they haven't been monitoring Fox News or MSNBC lately.

Something changes as an observer gets closer to the surface, however. It's when you drill down into a local view that the challenges are more visible. Why is that? What changes from the view from on high to the view on the ground where all the conflict takes place? How do we look like the United States of America to others outside our nation and look so disunited to ourselves? Well, we'll qualify that by saying we used to look like a cohesive nation until these last 50 years or so brought about more and deeper paradoxes.

So, let's look briefly at some of the other factors, starting with a quest to dominate political and governmental relationships. This will pull from Walt Natemeyer's Appendix A, The Essentials of Power and Influence. Walt's work lays out a tested and executable framework for exercising effective power relationships, given a workable understanding of power and influence. As Walt's work on Situational Leadership and Power, as well as Chapter 1 make clear, a power relationship works best when it's a two-way street, and even better when the leader and follower are in full agreement about their roles and responsibilities. Our goal for this and the next essay is to provide a way to think about Walt's explanations and paradox within a timely context that guides the future of our nation. That's what has made writing this current essay so challenging.

Quest for Political and Government Domination[63]

In this essay, the quest for domination in a relationship applies to the two main political parties— Republicans and Democrats. Since the days of John Adams and Thomas Jefferson's jockeying for control to be second President, factions, as Publius called them, have sought to be the controlling influence for our nation. The original battles these factions fought were largely between those favoring state's rights versus the federal government's influence. Interestingly, those concepts of states versus federal still provide the perceived causes for the Red-Blue scuffles we face today. But it runs much deeper than that.

Since the Nixon era, our main disconnectedness has depended on whether you view things through *our* nation's eyes or *my* nation's eyes.

It's even more than "we" and "me," however. It also reflects on the perspectives of "big" government versus "small" government, and progressivism versus conservatism, each of these manifesting in a quest for domination. The paradox of these disagreements, often out-and-out conflicts, is rooted in the fact that the power relationship between the two sides is routinely broken, perhaps throughout our entire history as a nation, but certainly in the past 50 years. Since politics exercise almost complete control over our governmental systems these days, we'll look mostly through the political lens.

The political **Paradoxes of Power** often sidetrack the entire endeavor to build "the more perfect union" and keep us from fulfilling the dreams of our Framers. Here are some perspective examples:

- In simple terms, *conservatism* looks at the present and probably too much to the past. One caveat is important, however: the following description is of a Republican party that may no longer exist since the 2016 election, or perhaps even since Nixon. The conservative movement prior to President Donald Trump sought to maintain the status quo, opting for individual and states' rights' freedoms over collective and federal authorities for the most part. In the main it was about reducing federal government authorities and expenditures, but it also spilled over into religious and moral objections to smaller groups that represented changing gender and racial issues. Conservatives feel such an approach may typically be less expensive to take in terms of government spending, but it produces a vision that can fail to anticipate and adapt to a rapidly changing future such as we face in 2020. Conservatism tends to view threats and opportunities in a reactive fashion and prefers not to act until it's necessary, or even after it's too late to make a meaningful difference. Smaller government and lower taxes should be sufficient to maintain the conservative lifestyle in their view, and "socialist" policies are anathema, except of course for Social Security and Medicare. In recent decades, conservatives have sought to bestow generous aid and tax breaks to corporate and business interests despite deficit concerns. Conservatism as practiced by today's Republican Party focuses on self-sufficiency and taking care of "me" as an individual, even to the point of considering corporations as "individuals" when it comes to exerting a role in campaign financing. In sum, the conservative movement in the US is about "me," "now" and searching for "the good old days" of the past.

When pondering American conservatism, think: Me and Mine, Now, Suspicion and Fear about Change, and Personal Freedom

- Conversely, **progressivism** looks at the world and anticipates change and societal upheaval. It seeks to prepare for the unfolding of multiple scenarios because while it relies on science and prediction, it also knows that prediction is inexact at best. This makes preparation expensive and requires more of a government role to oversee that preparation. Progressivism, or liberalism as it's sometimes called, embraces the "we" as a collective experience and investment target. Typically, no opportunity is too big for progressive government and "we" must prepare for the future no matter how it comes to pass. Science is a big deal and "we" must invest in the education and facilities that make good science possible. While self-sufficiency is important, progressives also lean towards collective success and opportunity. To be sure, the progressive movement has its share of inconsistencies and potential for abuse of ideals when they become the dominant force in politics. For example, in recent years, the Democratic party deemed it so important to get health care reform done while they had a filibuster-proof majority in the Senate and majority in the House in the first two years of

President Barack Obama's presidency, they felt they had to essentially "jam it down the throats" of the GOP. This didn't go over too well with the electorate and the Democrats lost the House of Representatives the very next election cycle after Obama's first two years in office. Their collective objectives don't always resonate with the voting public. Of course, one could argue that in the time of COVID-19, the Democrats' efforts on health care was a fortuitous effort on the part of the party. While we can debate whether the overall approach minimizes the quest for win-win outcomes, in sum progressivism is about "we," "the proper role of bigger, more inclusive government," "investment in the whole," and "looking towards better days." But in most cases, "we" tends to last "as long as 'you' agree with 'us'" which is one thing progressives appear to have in common with conservatives.

When pondering American Progressivism, think: We and Ours, Investment in the Future, Science, Inclusive Government and Collective Responsibility, and Sustainability

- A central paradox is that these general descriptions rarely fit either party any longer, Republican or Democrat. According to historian Andrew J. Bacevich, "Centered on consumption and individual autonomy, the (American) exercise of freedom is contributing to the gradual erosion of our national power...our reserves of power are being depleted." Bacevich addresses mainly national power but has something to say about Americans in general that still applies. "As individuals, Americans never cease to expect more. As members of a community, especially as members of a national community, they choose to contribute less."[64] Bacevich wrote this around 2008, long before Trump rode the escalator towards presidential fame. As a people, we were already disposed to withdraw from the international community, it seems. It may not matter which party claims our membership if greed, self-indulgence and isolation continue to drive our behavior as a nation.[65]

- It's also become increasingly clear that swinging back and forth between the domination of one movement over the other has damaged the United States dramatically both in terms of people and national treasure. The deep polarity between progressivism and conservativism brought on by self-serving, divisive politicians who seek only to elevate themselves and their party over united, national interests, is costing this nation dearly. Since we no longer seek what used to be called "The Happy Medium" we spend more money, fight more political wars, and delay planning and executing a sustainable future. Yes, power relationships in our nation are deeply fractured and only getting worse. **Paradoxes of Power** are everywhere you look.

All of this essentially means that no matter which party we claimed, Democrat or Republican, as a nation, we had already begun pulling away from the principles we once said were important in terms of international commitments and alliances. These principles were critical to the nation that led the Allies through WWII. The aftermath of the Cold War, however, left the two parties turning more and more inward and even the progressives began losing an interest in collective experiences that didn't benefit those of their own kind. The quest for political domination only worsened these trends. The "we" became the stricter definition of those with whom we agreed specifically, and the power grabs for domination escalated. This particularly applied to domestic issues, thus, the nation was ripe for Trump's "outsider" revolution in government. Beginning primarily with Reagan, accompanied by Lee Atwater's implementation of the Southern Strategy,[66] the divisions that have split our nation in 2020 have left us in a significant **Paradox of Power** where power relationships have broken down completely.

In essence, there have been substantial failures in leadership on both sides. The Left's demonization of white working class as racist, sexist, and unwilling to become educated[67] enabled the

Republican party to systematically pick up traditional Democrats such as the Southern Democrats, the Reagan Democrats (more Democrats in the South, working-class Democrats in the North), and finally, the Trump Democrats (working-class Democrats left behind by their party and Independents fed up with Washington and coastal elites).[68] The Left's inability to solve problems of crime and poverty in cities made things both effectively and visually worse. In addition, the conservative mobilization of the working class, accompanied by failure to protect through excessive deregulation, and now failed leadership on COVID-19, has greatly weakened the perceptions of strength the so-called traditional GOP formerly enjoyed.

The problem in both cases is that elites in either political wing are willing to mobilize common people for votes and power but have failed to do much for them. It's massively confusing to the electorate and therefore particularly challenging to maintain loyalty to either party. We think the Founders might address that today by saying: "The balance of factions is okay...we understand that with this much diversity and this many people in the nation that we can't always agree about everything. But for God's sake, please be loyal to our founding principles of freedom and opportunity for all, and for all who would become Americans. Be loyal to the **United** States of America first... please."

From this fundamental discussion on the quest for political power, we'll next turn to education as the next great hope to lift us out of the morass of politics and government we've created for ourselves. First, however, we must understand the paradoxes we've created in that endeavor too.

The Many Paradoxes of Education[69]

The Founders of our nation realized that an informed electorate would be critical for the nation's success.[70] Paradoxically federal, state, and local governments have paid little attention to the return on investment in education, particularly for minorities. The shortcomings are somewhat understandable because of the highly distributed nature of educational systems at the various levels that oversee where children learn about their world and their nation. The two ruling political parties generally agree that education is necessary and useful, but their visions have differed in the utility of funding it to the level that keeps the United States at the top of the heap compared to other nations.

With its exacerbated financial crisis in the nation, education has fallen under its own **Paradoxes of Power**. The roots of these paradoxes run deep and undergird much of the skepticism and resentment of "elite expertise" we see today. For so many immigrants in a society of immigrants, education was the ticket to freedom and prosperity. The first generation of immigrants labored hard in the hopes that their offspring would get an education and have a better life. Andrew Carnegie, an American elitist "Captain of Industry," ironically institutionalized this process. While exploiting the labor of mainly Irish and East European immigrants in his 19th Century steel mills, he famously built libraries across the nation so their children could have a better life through education. However, education remained a two-tier system that dated back to ancient Greek and Roman times – basic skills for the working class and critical thinking skills for the ruling class.

World War II upset this system that was convenient for the elite. The G.I. Bill was one way the nation rewarded the sacrifices of the 16 million Americans who saved the nation and the world from fascism. It opened higher education to the masses and led to an unprecedented growth in universities. When the Soviets surprised the West by launching the first satellite into space, the U.S. government responded with a massive K-12 science education program, the establishment of DARPA (the Defense Advanced Research Projects Agency), and eventually the National Science Foundation (NSF) to support all sciences. These developments were a boon to the expansion of education, opportunity, the physical, biological, and social sciences, and freedom of thought.[71] Unfortunately, unforeseen events would derail this system, and some of our society's most cherished principles would help to undermine it.

As the U.S. rolled from a hot war against fascism into a Cold War against communism, the nation was trying to throw off the yoke of Jim Crow laws (see Chapter 8) and racism that restricted the freedoms of Black Americans. The Cold War and fight against racism led to the politically divisive Vietnam War and battle for civil rights respectively. College campuses became hotbeds of dissent and protest over both issues. Universities have always been crucibles for controversy. The first acknowledged academic, Socrates, was accused of "corrupting the youth of Athens" and was executed for it over 2500 years ago. The concepts of academic freedom and tenure were developed in the Middle Ages to protect professors from censorship, loss of employment or worse from authorities who objected to controversial teachings (Fuchs, 1963). In the 1500's coffee shops in Mecca were outlawed because imams feared thoughts fomented by academics over cups of caffeine.[72] Controversy is no stranger to the college campus, nor should it be! However, when even well-intentioned and noble principles become hardened into inviolate truths, the educational enterprise is paradoxically undermined.

Our nation is founded on freedom of thought and speech. However, the expansive American university system created a new hierarchy of intellectual haves and have-nots (Kerr, 1991). As the essayists, despite our having PhDs and being great admirers of higher education, we argue that this system has failed. Education became a new hierarchy and political litmus tests increasingly became the price of admission. The result is a new **Paradox of Power**, the creation of fractured, dysfunctional campuses, and the unintentional creation of an intellectual elite versus a demeaned working class. Perhaps a necessary corollary to our Declaration of Independence's claim that "all men are created equal" is that all men equally die and what happens in between makes no difference in the quality of the "man" whether well-educated or not.[73]

Our critique of American education is only just beginning. Emerging out of 1960s protests, radical academics used Paul Feyerabend's (1975) philosophical work to argue against the existence of reality, enabling people to create their own realities with no regard to the world around them. Saul Alinskey urged university students to favor tactics of physical confrontation over reasoned debate and engagement with the political system.[74] Academic advocates of social justice for women, minorities, and the poor turned away from embracing the objective analysis of evidence to imposing their own realities on others (Gross & Levitt, 1994; Harris, 1999; Kuznar, 2009; Sidky, 2003, 2018). Well-intentioned programs where badly needed scholarship on issues of minorities and women can be supported have instead become a balkanized landscape of "culture studies" programs myopically focused on advocating for specific interest groups (ethnic minorities, feminists, various dimensions of sexual orientation). Though their existence holds the promise of shining a light on neglected lives, they too often turn into forums where like-minded professors and students reinforce one-another's worldviews.

One paradox of the explosion of these programs is that they effectively ghettoize their interest groups and issues. University administrators get to demonstrate their support for a special interest group by having the program, those in the program get to feel justified in reinforcing their identities, and the rest of the student body and faculty more or less go on with their academic lives, never really having to learn about women and various minorities and the issues that impact their lives... the paradoxes continue to grow and leadership functions cause greater damage to power relationships.

This intellectual balkanization can take particularly toxic

forms. An incident during the birth of the Black Lives Matter movement in 2015 illustrates the point. BLM protestors occupied a common area on the University of Missouri campus and ironically denied press access. A student journalist, Tim Tai, attempted to conduct interviews when a white professor of communication tried to forcibly remove him, turning to Black male students and asking, "Who wants to help me get this reporter out of here? I need some muscle over here."[75] While she later apologized for her actions in that moment, there could be nothing more paradoxical than a white, privileged radical academic ordering Black men to rough up an Asian-American student journalist; the right-wing media had a field day with it and our country was further divided. In the moment, the professor felt personally justified but clearly overrode the common good. Notably, none of the Black American men answered her call, their integrity overruled the white professor's (and wielder of power) command, a lesson for us all.

This incident brings us back to the point that academics have helped to create the political divides in our society and inadvertently became pawns of the political right. Icons of civil disobedience such as Dr. Martin Luther King and the recently departed Representative John Lewis, championed the power of civil disobedience, "lovingly violating the law," and engaging in "good trouble." They knew how to agitate peacefully for and achieve change without playing into the hands of their adversaries. This lesson is tragically lost on academics today. The Ivory Tower is tarnished with the same intolerance it originally intended to abolish, reinforcing conservative perceptions summarized in the following way by former Attorney General Jeff Sessions:

The American university was once the center of academic freedom —a place of robust debate, a forum for the competition of ideas. But it is transforming into an echo chamber of political correctness and homogenous thought, a shelter for fragile egos (Sessions, 2017).

Even when not being overtly political, the biases of many academics subvert their own honest attempts at objective research. Noted political scientist Phil Tetlock (1994) provided a damning assessment in an article subtitled, "Is the road to scientific hell paved with good moral intentions?" A proponent of robust social science, Tetlock noted how the hypotheses social scientists test are typically set up to preserve their political viewpoints. "Scientific Hell" occurs when the policy makers social scientists wish to influence actually dismiss their research because it is perceived as biased. In more recent years, US Naval War College professor Tom Nichols describes how this has contributed to the widespread skepticism he calls the "Death of Expertise" and how it is exploited in divisive ways by politicians.[76]

Universities should be hallowed centers of learning and the pursuit of truth and justice. None of these can be achieved without research that probes issues that make us uncomfortable and engenders robust debate. Furthermore, true learning is not possible without the ability to admit fault; one has to be able to admit one does not know or one's ideas are wrong in order to replace them with expanded knowledge and new ideas. This is not possible without being able to say, "I'm sorry. I was wrong." Unfortunately, those words are rarely uttered on college campuses today.[77] Generating the truly informed electorate the Founders thought was essential to democracy is paradoxically impossible under current conditions. This is a true **Paradox of Power**.

And what of those who do not attain the credentials of a university degree? They stand very much on the outside and in profoundly disadvantaged positions. Holders of university degrees make on average over 15 thousand dollars a year more than those with high school degrees. During the Great Recession of 2009, unemployment among those without a college degree was 15%, while it was 5% for those with a college degree. And during the COVID-19 pandemic, it was the retail clerks, garbage collectors, cooks, and skilled crafts persons that everyone, including the educated elite, suddenly found "essential," and who then labored at great personal risk to provide people with their basic needs. Not passing the university bar leaves one materially disadvantaged and in some ways worse, socially devalued (Campbell, 2018; Vance, 2016).

The divide of educational haves and have-nots overlaps with the nation's political divides, encouraging politicians to look down upon the have-nots as "deplorables" or dismiss credentialed experts as just a bunch of "smart people" who neither know what they are talking about nor care about the common man.[78] We have seen this trend accelerated by the COVID-19 pandemic, which has pitted our nation's top medical experts against others who promote unsubstantiated cures, deny non-pharmaceutical interventions such as mask wearing, and believe that reproductive disorders are caused by having sex with demons in one's dreams.[79]

When those in educational power, the professoriate, double down on their political positions, use their classrooms as bully pulpits for imposing their views on captive audiences of students, force one another to uphold views that cannot be questioned, and then take those not in their club for granted or worse, demean them, then the campus has become a paradox indeed and unfortunately resembles the echo chamber described in former Attorney General Sessions' remarks. And wielders of power, left or right, who wish to divide a nation for their own personal gain and against the common good, are empowered because there will be plenty of yielders primed to accept their message. These actions may be among the longest lasting, most systemic and destructive **Paradoxes of Power** we face in our nation.

When educational paradoxes interact with the political paradoxes, we're left defenseless to overcome the greatest threats we face as a society of freedom- and opportunity-loving people. Well, that is except perhaps for the challenges of a justice system that refuses to look at each offender through the same, impartial lens and relies on religious beliefs to guide thought in even the most secular environments—our government. The next chapter tackles those very thorny paradoxes.

References Cited

Alinsky, S. D. (1946). *Reveille for Radicals*. Chicago: University of Chicago Press.

Campbell, J. L. (2018). *American Discontent: The Rise of Donald Trump and the Decline of the Golden Age*. Oxford: Oxford University Press.

Feyerabend, P. (1975). *Against Method*. London: New Left Books.

Fuchs, R. F. (1963). Academic Freedom -- Its Basic Philosophy, Function, and History. *Articles by Maurer Faculty, 1634*, 431-446.

Gross, P., & Levitt, N. (1994). *Higher Superstition*. Baltimore: Johns Hopkins University Press.

Harris, M. (1999). *Theories of Culture in Postmodern Times*. Walnut Creek, California: Altamira Press.

Keeley, L. H. (1996). *War before Civilization: The Myth of the Peaceful Savage*. Oxford: Oxford University Press.

Kerr, C. (1991). The Great Transformation in Higher Education 1960-1980.

Kuznar, L. A. (2009). *Reclaiming a Scientific Anthropology, Second Edition*. Walnut Creek, California: AltaMira Press.

Pinker, S. (2011). *The Better Angels of Our Nature: Why Violence Has Declined*. New York: Penguin.

Sessions, J. (2017). Talk on Free Speech at Georgetown Law, September 26, 2017. In.

Sidky, H. (2003). *A Critique of Postmodern Anthropology: In Defense of Disciplinary Origins and Traditions*. Lewiston, New York: Edwin Mellen Press.

Sidky, H. (2018). The War on Science, Anti-Intellectualism, and'Alternative Ways of Knowing' in 21st-Century America. *Skeptical Inquirer, 42*(2). Retrieved from https://www.csicop.org/si/show/e_war_on_science_anti-intellectualism_and_alternative_ways_of_knowing_in_21

Tetlock, P. (1994). Political psychology or politicized psychology: Is the road to scientific hell paved with good moral intentions? *Political Psychology, 15*(3), 509-530.

Vance, J. D. (2016). *Hillbilly Elegy: A Memoir of a Family and Culture in Crisis*. New York: Harper.

8. Religion And Justice As Paradoxes Of Power

by Carl W. Hunt and Lawrence A. Kuznar[80]

As we noted in Chapter 7 on Government and Education, these American systems were informed by a scientific foundation inculcated with our values. Our new form of government emerged in the throes of the Age of the Enlightenment, a time when reason and science were informing so much of the western world, and our definitions of government and education reflected that. There are two other areas central to most peoples' lives, however, where that relationship is flipped: religion and justice. These two topics, also critical to our founding, are based on ideals that didn't necessarily reject science and reason, but they were not central to it. In this chapter we examine how even our most sacred institutions are not immune to **Paradoxes of Power**.

Paradoxes in Religion[81]

We have only a modest bit to write about the function of religion in the United States, not because it isn't important but because we feel we should follow the example of the Framers and the US Constitution, notably Article VI and the First Amendment.[82] Namely, in the final summary of our founding documents, religious belief is a matter between an individual American and his or her divine inspiration, if there is one. Our Founders, some of whom were devout and forthcoming believers in God, such as George Washington and John Adams, and some of whom were less active declarants, such as Thomas Jefferson and James Madison, all agreed that the United States should enable but not enthusiastically support religious influence and activity. Our first four presidents, all of whom had major roles in our founding, were firm in both their personal beliefs and the role they felt religion would have in our nation despite adherence to their respective faiths.

Nonetheless, religion plays a significant, sometimes outsized role in our social life and we feel we must recognize its influence in the development and implementation of power relationships in our nation.[83] When these power relationships malfunction, as they often do when religion is involved, people, organizations and even our nation suffer from a **Paradox of Power**. We propose to address religion and its role in contributing to paradoxes through a few simple lines of inquiry intended to provoke thought more than take a firm position on any of the questions below. We expect to practice the same philosophy as our Founders...the less said the better. However, we believe we have to say something, even if only in the form of a few questions.

If our goal is to convince our future generations of America to think for themselves and challenge our nation to be better, using thoughtful inquiry to assist people to form their own beliefs and philosophies seems prudent. We're not going to tell you what to think or believe, but we will challenge you to ask yourselves what you believe and why. It's as important to understand this now as it was at the founding of our nation. As our 34th President, Dwight D. Eisenhower, famously (perhaps infamously at the time) said "(i)n other words, our form of government has no sense unless it is founded in a deeply felt religious faith, and I don't care what it is."[84]

Religion has played and continues to play a significant role in this nation, as it has in almost every nation in history. Just because you may not agree with the tenets or "laws" of a religious movement other than your own, however, does not mean it's evil, disloyal or dangerous to our nation, or even wrong. It just means our nation is founded on the principles of religious freedom, and as Ike said, "I don't care what it is."

When pondering the function of religion and resultant paradoxes in our nation and in your own life, ask yourself the following:

- Why is religion important to me? What do I seek from a relationship with my God or my faith?

- Is my faith or my religious movement better than someone
else's? Why do I think that?

- Should I receive special treatment from the government or
someone else because I am a believer in a certain faith movement? What motivates me to feel that way? What about
other peoples' religions?

- Should my church attempt to insert itself in government
policy or law?

- What responsibilities to my nation, my community, my
family or my friends do I have as a believer in my God or my
faith? What if I don't believe in a God or faith; what are my responsibilities to my nation?

Here are some questions directed at the Evangelical Movements in particular:

- Does your faith require tolerance for and acceptance of all
people? If so, how does one reconcile the intolerance and big-
otry that exists against people of different origins, persuasions and beliefs? Matthew 25:35[85]

- Why do we continue to put into office anti-immigrant politicians when our entire nation is built on the strength of
immigrants? How do we reconcile this sort hypocrisy, which
is condemned by Jesus himself in Matthew 23:23? Is this not
paradoxical in the extreme?[86], [87]

- Donald Trump owes much of his support to the Evangelical
community despite the paradoxes Christians face in assess-

ing the personal character of this president. A recent collection of essays by Evangelical Christians documents the challenges they face and yet many Evangelicals reportedly still intend to vote for someone who has repeatedly flaunted Christian values throughout his life.[88] Do voting Christians put politics before principle and character? How much greater evidence should they need to witness before realizing the damage done to their personal character, their nation and indeed to their faith by continuing to support this president and those who have enabled him to represent them as a leader of America?

- Are these questions you feel your faith requires you to address?

Addressing questions such as these honestly and directly should help us understand the potential for abuse of religiously motivated power relationships between us and others, as well as us and our nation. Power is not necessarily secular nor is it divine, except how it motivates and inspires us to be the best individual contributor to family or community, friends or nation. We should leverage the power which religion instills in us to be better, not to dominate. Otherwise, we foster and promote paradoxes everywhere we go, within every organization we serve. Think about that as you answer the questions above and others that come to mind about **Paradoxes of Power**.

In order to be fully objective, we also need to consider that religion and faith in any deity can be a paradox, as well. To people who do not believe in any god, one of the biggest paradoxes of the power of religion is that any "power" it instills in people, whether they be leaders or followers, is based on faith and belief alone. Speaking purely scientifically, it's challenging to demonstrate empirical data to support the existence of any god or other spiritual entity apart from the "evidence" we accept as a result of religious beliefs. When we feel close to God, that's a feeling generated from within and given how many religious faiths there are in our world, there are a lot of generated feelings, each different in their own way.

A non-believing person could cite the following example: a Pharaoh in ancient Egypt walks up to a crowd and say "Hey guys, check it out, I'm a God." And then instead of the people asking "Why" or saying "Okay, but prove it," they just respond with an "Okay, cool, I guess we better worship you then." That seems like a Paradox of Power in that you would expect people to question a claim like that. Is such an example that different from how many religious leaders conduct themselves today and indeed throughout history? We may all claim a relationship with God, including the authors of this essay, but that could also indicate paradox itself. For the Christian, perhaps that's why 1 Thessalonians 5:21 advises believers, "But examine everything carefully; hold fast to that which is good."[89] Other translations say to "test all things" …wise advice indeed.

Power Paradoxes of Justice in America[90]

It's tempting to seek to provoke thought about Justice and Paradox in America using primarily the same inquiry technique as above. After all, inquiry challenges us all to ask our own questions and to form our own assessments, what some call hypotheses, about the things we seek and learn. But it's worth making a few points about Justice and **Paradoxes of Power** first. Honest inquiry throughout our lives can drive true discovery and learning if we pay attention to how we frame our questions. Nowhere else is that truer than when we interrogate the systems of justice we honor and employ in the United States.

Recall that we said in Chapter 1 and reinforced through all the essays that a Paradox of Power is a malfunction of the power relationship that occurs between leaders and followers, wielders of and yielders to power. It takes place when a person or organization exercises authority in a way that reduces the potential of the group as a whole. This means it's primarily a leadership malfunction, although occasionally followers also provoke a paradox, as Walt Natemeyer discusses in Appendix A. Systems of justice suffer from the same potential paradoxes, whether brought on by people, rules or society.

Author Mychal Denzel Smith writes in the September 2020 Atlantic Magazine, "It's important here to define justice, as the U.S. legal system has perverted our sense of it. It cannot be punishment or retribution for harm caused. Justice is not revenge. Rather, justice is a proactive commitment to providing each person with the material and social conditions in which they can both survive and thrive as a healthy and self-actualized human being."[91] Smith tells us both what justice is and what it is not in a powerful statement about power relationships involving law enforcement officials and the public they are sworn to protect. "...it requires all of us to buy into the idea that we must take responsibility for one another. But it is the only form of a just world," Smith noted. This is the essence of good power relationships between leaders and followers, and it's the front line for those who enforce justice policy as it's practiced in the US—law enforcement.

In America, we have a system of justice that's empowered by various provisions of the Constitution, including Sections 7 and 8 of Article I, Section 2 and 3 of Article II, and of course, Article III, as well as various provisions of other parts of the Constitution, including Amendments. The point is that our justice system involves all parts of our federal government and is similarly reflected in state and local governments. Justice is a holistic effort of American government and the policy it enacts. We are all involved, and we are all affected by the actions of the various functions of our system of justice in this nation. We all have a stake in it, and we all must constantly monitor it to ensure we or others don't abuse justice...that we don't abuse the power relationships between each other.

Our Founders originally intended that justice would be served equitably to all American citizens. Of course, it took them and their political progeny a while to realize that "all Americans" extends beyond white property-owning males, but we eventually arrived for the most part. While justice in America has always been inconsistently applied, even today, there is no legal basis for these inconsistencies...that's the truth we must admit to change things and make justice work for all Americans.

We tend to think of justice in America as the "criminal justice" system, but really, it's far more than that, as Smith observes in his <u>Atlantic</u> piece. It's an entire system that enables success for all. Justice in America, in theory, provides equal access to all the benefits to which every American has access as a citizen. It involves the creation and sustainment of a construct that empowers every American to succeed, or at a minimum, it doesn't constrain Americans from access to these opportunities for success. Such constraints on Americans would indeed be a **Paradox of Power**, and paradoxically, this condition was baked into American justice from the beginning.

Let's begin to think about that now, through a handful of short, initial questions:

- How is justice supposed to work in America? When it fails, why doesn't justice work consistently?

- What are the systemic paradoxes that exist to prevent justice from working consistently for all Americans? What's baked into American Justice that provides potential for abuse? What's baked into American justice that can be used to overcome abuse?

- What's necessary to mitigate or overcome policy misuses and abuses that codify our mistakes so that justice might be uniformly administered across the nation? How do we make justice fair?

- Where do we start to correct our justice shortcomings? If it's more than one place, where do we find the leverage points to provide uniformity across all levels of government? What have been useful sparks in the past to fix justice shortcomings and how does that help us see what needs to be done now?

- What are the best public faces for these changes: police officers, elected officials, teachers, citizen activists? How do we "sell" these critically needed changes to the public so that truly equal justice becomes the norm rather than the exception...so that rich people might not have access to better justice than those without wealth?

These kinds of questions point to why we brought up religion before justice. Individual beliefs are related to individual actions which in turn relate to collective beliefs and actions. If greed, hatred and thirst for power drive individual thoughts and desires, these elements eventually affect and focus collective behavior. Our Founders understood the impulses of some to invent ideologies and supporting movements, such as religions and political parties, to justify collective behaviors and personal greed. Our Founders realized those temptations and attempted to set up a government that might somehow temper the individual before he or she could influence collective behavior. It didn't work out that way completely, and at best it was a well-meaning start. Smith's definition of justice, above, helps to change thinking and sustain that start into something with longevity, if we can embrace it.

Perhaps our biggest problem is that we collectively climb on the "Bus to Abilene" whenever we begin to correct the flaws of the Founders' original work and succeeding attempts to fix our justice system.[92] Over time, we've forgotten to challenge ourselves with the kinds of questions we asked above, even when correcting recognized flaws. We typically address only a recently noticed failing in the justice system and fail to correct the underlying reasons why justice is not provided fairly and across the board in our nation. We mistakenly rely on a system of justice that tasks courts, up to and including the US Supreme

Court, to correct these failings in a so-called systemic fashion, but the people on those courts rarely go back and challenge themselves with those questions. When this happens, the justice system enters a state of paradox and fails to repair the underlying issues that resulted in the abuse of power in the first place; this is typically a biased or narrowly applied law. To further the paradox, we fail to hold the legislative or regulatory process and people accountable for enacting these inappropriate laws and regulations.

It appears if we really understood the principles that much religious inspiration was developed for—to overcome greed, covetousness, hatred, and dishonesty—we might apply the general philosophy to justice, as well. It seems the Founders at least weighed that as they embarked upon the great experiment that is America. We should also consider, by the way, the following: the United States of America is still an experiment, and we are still learning from it. The problem is that we rarely seem to incorporate what we learn, particularly when it comes to justice in this nation. Maybe the problem is that we forget what we learned, and our still young institutions just don't know how to make the most of our "education."

Paradoxes of Power in the American justice system include some of the following (a superficial list to be sure):

1. <u>Law enforcement</u>.[93] Most Americans relate to their ideas of justice in America through interactions with the uniformed police officer on the street, or what they see in the news or police TV dramas. This forms an emotionally-based power relationship with American justice that negates the richer definition that Smith articulates in his article above. Because of this, we think of the abuse of authority in law enforcement, using what appears to be *excessive* force to make arrests, and then rationalizing why that level of force was needed.[94] It also includes relying on a police union or sympathetic city government to bail out the offending officers when they make mistakes or

commit outright abuses of power, justifying that their cops "are the best in the world," "can't make willful mistakes" and "need our full support." We saw some first-hand examples of that in Dennis Greene's essay in Chapter 4. Also, in Chapter 4, Marc Hill's essay comments on what excessive force can mean in peaceful protests, given his first-hand experiences being on the receiving end of it.

While working as a radio patrol officer in Houston in the early 1970s, I too noticed the tendency of senior law enforcement officers and city officials to automatically take the side of the cop on the street and systems were in place to keep the apparent offenders "innocent" as long as possible. After years of serving in the military, where I felt there was a more neutral system of leadership, I see that tendency as misguided, placing too much authority in the hands of police unions and laws that protect officers through "qualified immunity." The idea of "protect and serve," the motto of many police departments, has to mean more than "self-protect and self-serve" to instill confidence in our justice system. The same inertia applies to law enforcement enforcers at all levels, including bureaucrats and even elected officials such as county sheriffs, and only the same election process can remove offenders. We submit that these are **Paradoxes of Power** that have been too long perpetuated in the American justice system.

Finally, an additional paradox occurs when the police are outfitted in equipment that is clearly military assault gear, including heavy-wheeled armored vehicles we've seen on televised reports in past years. Even more recently, we've observed the clearly inappropriate use of unidentified forces and tactics in cities such as Washington, DC and Portland, OR. Certainly, police officers on the front line must have appropriate protection in violent protest situations, but these officials must also weigh the inflammatory nature of militarized equipment and tactics that aggravate demonstrations above the minimum level of force needed to quell or stabilize these situations. Sending in military equipment and using military tactics designed for combat operations, particularly as an initial action, will in too many cases elevate the protests far beyond what was intended by either side. Again, we want to avoid encouraging either side from climbing "on the bus to Abilene."

2. <u>Justice Enforcement</u>: This is an example of willful misinterpretation or violation of a law or rule that is intended to protect all or some constituents, such as what we've traditionally classified as minorities, itself a contrived classification; all Americans are Americans, regardless of race or gender. Most people would likely prefer not to be considered minorities and would rather be Americans first, with equal access to all the benefits and responsibilities that all Americans possess. As a general note, this section applies specifically to politicians and law makers, whereas the preceding paragraph applied to law enforcers.

John Stuart Mill in *On Liberty* wrote, "The only purpose for which power can be rightfully exercised over any member of a civilized community against his will is to prevent harm to others."[95] Mill's philosophy became the root of what we call "majority rule with minority rights," a fundamental tenant of democracy that greatly influenced the way our Founders thought of our "more perfect union" as the preamble of our Constitution proclaims. But as we've noted, our Constitution did not get it all right the first time around and thus offered a way to amend mistakes as we grew as a nation. The Founders also knew factions...political parties...would form and find ways to divide thought and action in our nation, thus dividing our population.

Generously speaking, when politicians only appeal to segments of the population, they (hopefully) unwittingly divide this nation. They propose policies and laws that favor some subset of the nation in order to "correct" some past error in lawmaking, judgment or execution (see previous section). Politicians and ultimately lawmakers must live with or overcome the policies of previous generations of lawmakers and so we hope they continue down this path with the benign intent to correct past injustices. However, if our current generations of lawmakers are restricted only to fixing the errors of the past, it's increasingly difficult to focus on the future and of a more holistic perspective of systematic justice as Smith describes in his <u>Atlantic</u> essay. More **Paradoxes of Power**, to be sure.

3. <u>Unequal interpretation or application of law</u> in a courtroom or government administration office to show antipathy to a person or group of people against whom the authority harbors biases or grudges. This is one of the most heinous **Paradoxes of Power** in that it displays outright disdain for the equitable rule of law, and for which there is no justification.

The United States has a long list of miscarriages of justice in which laws were not equally applied, often on the basis of prejudice. We offer a few examples to make the point. Regrettably, the list of Black men falsely accused of raping white women is a long trail of injustice that weaves its way through our nation's history. The "Scottsboro Boys" case eventually reached the U.S. Supreme Court and led to the requirement that Blacks cannot be convicted by all-white juries (Bellamy, 2014; Klarman, 2009). In 1931, a mixed group of Black and White poor youth were hitching a ride on a freight train in Alabama. A confrontation broke out when the Whites declared the train "White Only" and to tried push nine Black teenagers (aged 12-19) off the train. The White youths lost the fight and laid charges with the police. Two White women were also on the train, and when the sheriff arrested the Black youths, the women claimed they had been raped by them. A medical examination was performed and found no evidence of rape. As word spread that a group of Black men raped two White women, a lynch mob formed. The sheriff courageously confronted the mob and phoned the Governor who fortunately sent the Alabama National Guard to protect the accused. A number of miscarriages of justice followed, however, including rushed trials and prejudiced juries.

Despite two United States Supreme Court over-rulings, eight of the men were eventually convicted (Klarman, 2009). They served varying terms, most eventually paroled, but their lives had been altered forever. The miscarriage was so severe that even segregationist Alabama Governor George Wallace officially pardoned one of the men in 1976. In 2013, the Alabama Supreme Court officially pardoned all the accused.

Prejudice leading to unequal application of the law is not only a product of the Jim Crow (see below) South. In 1989, a large group of Black and Latino men spontaneously gathered in New York City's Central Park to rob and beat people. A 28-year old White investment banker was raped, beaten, and left to die in a coma that evening. The New York City police rounded up five Black and Latino youths, aged 14-16, and interrogated them without representation, and coerced confessions (Johnson, 2005). Meanwhile, a medical examiner found no match between DNA on the victim and the teenagers, and later, each of them recanted their confessions. However, public opinion was inflamed, stoked by then real estate mogul Donald Trump who on May 1, 1989, published full-page ads in The New York Times, The Daily News, The New York Post, and New York Newsday calling for the death penalty for the accused. Eventually, they were all convicted and sent to prison and served between 5 and 13 years in prison. In 2002 the actual perpetrator, imprisoned for a string of rapes and a murder, confessed to the crime and his DNA confirmed his guilt. The fact that innocent Black men are still being prejudged and even killed for perceived threats to certain portions of the white population, demonstrates that our society has continued to perpetrate these kinds of abuses of justice.

4. The passing of laws intended to restrict the rights of targeted groups. After the emancipation of slaves and the end of the Civil War, whites in the South mobilized to suppress the new-found freedoms of Black Americans. This mobilization included terrorism and the emergence of the Ku Klux Klan, the

passing of laws designed to restrict the civil rights and political participation of Blacks, segregation of Whites and Blacks in everything from drinking fountains, to bus seats, to schools, and the glorification of the South's cause during the Civil War. The height of these developments was between the 1870s and the mid-1950s and has been dubbed the Jim Crow era after an 1800s racist depiction of Black slaves. This was an era filled with tens of thousands of lynchings, violent suppression of voting rights, and the levying of poll taxes (having to pay to vote), all designed to intimidate and disenfranchise Blacks.[96]

American history presents so many examples of injustice against Blacks, but any group perceived as outsiders has experienced "legalized" forms of injustice. The immigration of Chinese to the United States in the 1800s eventually lead to the Chinese Exclusion Act of 1882, which prohibited Chinese immigration and led to the massacres of dozens of Chinese in attempts to drive them out of the American West. Prejudice against the Irish and non-English speaking southern and eastern European immigrants in the early 1900s resulted in the passing of a series of immigration acts to require knowledge of English and established quotas limiting the number of immigrants from any country. In the past 30 years, immigration has emerged as a key and divisive political issue, with repeated attempts by congress to reform U.S. immigration law, failing because of a lack of leadership and reasonable compromise on both the right and left, and an issue used by politicians to mobilize political support (Suedfeld, Morrison, & Kuznar, 2020).

5. The misuse and abuse of power to protect the "greed, covetousness, hatred, and dishonesty" we described above. Protecting a **Paradox of Power**, once an authority realizes it exists, is unjustifiable and unsustainable in a nation that considers itself free and independent. The history of any society is replete with stories of the misuse of power in the service of greed, and we like to think that the United States is less so than most. However, we are not perfect and examining our own failings in this

area serves as another reminder of how **Paradoxes of Power** defeat our larger purpose. We offer the following examples where greed overruled a sustainable benefit to the collective, to the detriment of all.

ENRON was a Wall Street darling, a company that began as an energy company in 1985 and wound up being a highly profitable investment firm. However, its leadership colluded to take on risky investments, hiding billions in debts from their shareholders and reaping hundreds of millions in personal gains. Eventually, a courageous company vice-president, Sharron Watkins, exposed the fraud to federal authorities, and ENRON's house of cards came tumbling down. It was a difficult choice to make. Forgoing riches for herself, she knew her decision would hurt many honest hard-working employees in the short-run; in the end she knew she had to expose a corrupt inner circle to maintain the system of economic justice our society relies upon. She brought down some of the wealthiest and most powerful people in American business, not out of personal gain, but of dedication to a system of laws we all depend upon. ENRON is an example of a **Paradox of Power** and redemption.

The Great Recession of 2008 unfortunately does not appear to have the same heroic silver lining as our ENRON example. That recession began in the United States, fueled by unregulated greed and reverberated throughout the global economy. In the U.S., 6.2% of people lost their jobs, and economies around the world experienced recessions. The cause of this strife was predatory loans; these are housing loans extended to people who the lenders know cannot make payments, all so the lenders can pocket commissions for making their deals. It is a system that rewards greed at the expense of the indebted clients, the stakeholders who underwrite the loans, and the entire financial system. The ultimate result was financial ruin for many working-class and poor people and an unprecedented transfer of wealth to the top 1% (Gottschalk & Vornovitsky, 2012; Kuznar, Kuznar, & Aviles, 2019; Saez, 2013; Vornovitsky, Gottschalk, &

Smith, 2011; Wolff, 2016). However, this catastrophe had ripple effects and unintentionally fueled further political division in our country. Those who lost the most tended to blame the elite intellectual class, creating a backlash against the government at large and especially against highly educated and often liberal experts (Campbell, 2018; Economist Intelligence Unit, 2017; Majmunder, 2017; Sidky, 2018; Suedfeld et al., 2020). This backlash has further divided our society and created an even more dysfunctional government, ultimately incapable of responding adequately to the current challenge of the COVID-19 pandemic. A **Paradox of Power** in the economic realm led to multiple **Paradoxes of Power** in politics, and arguably the deaths of many Americans. Our observation is that the Millennial and perhaps younger generations of America and the West may never fully recover from the fallout of back-to-back recessions and depressed salaries.

You can see just by these limited examples, our justice system has a lot of opportunity to make a difference for America because these things and many like them happen routinely at every level of government and within our entire society. When we as individual citizens or residents turn away from these behaviors, allowing these behaviors to be "out of sight, out of mind," as essayist Joshua Hunt labels it, we are fostering and even supporting such paradoxes. Yet, we all do it and rationalize away our own behaviors. This is paradoxical indeed because we all contribute to malfunctions in the power relationships our Founders intended for our great experiment in constitutional democracy. We all suffer from the results.

We included thoughts on Religion and Justice in this collection of essays because we realized these are the two human endeavors that might also resolve the paradoxes we've wrought upon ourselves in this nation. From the time of WWII to the Nixon years, the US enjoyed general admiration from Western nations and even a growing number of other countries seeking to replicate the balance of power, freedom, security and opportunity America has enjoyed. Beginning with Nixon's abuses we highlighted in Chapter 7 we have begun a decline in that level of appreciation that has been accelerating ever since. Some of our leaders have tried to rescue us and some have simply let the status quo continue. It's the ones who made things worse that have placed our nation at such grave risk. Unfortunately for our nation, it appears our current president and his enablers fall into the latter category.

Chapters 9 and 10 will begin to explore just how we pull ourselves as individuals and as a nation from some of the greatest **Paradoxes of Power** we've ever experienced. We've pulled ourselves back from the brink before and with the power of good thinking and new energy that our youngest generations bring to our nation, we will put ourselves on the right track again.

References Cited

Bellamy, J. (2014). The Scottsboro Boys: Injustice in Alabama. *Prologue, Journal of the National Archives*(Spring 2014), 26-34. Retrieved from https://www.archives.gov/files/publications/prologue/2014/spring/scottsboro.pdf

Campbell, J. L. (2018). *American Discontent: The Rise of Donald Trump and the Decline of the Golden Age*. Oxford: Oxford University Press.

Economist Intelligence Unit. (2017). *Democracy Index 2016: Revenge of the "Deplorables."* Retrieved from http://www.eiu.com/public/topical_report.aspx?campaignid=DemocracyIndex2016

Gottschalk, A., & Vornovitsky, M. (2012). Changes in Household Net Worth from 2005 to 2010. Retrieved from https://www.census.gov/newsroom/blogs/random-samplings/2012/06/changes-in-household-net-worth-from-2005-to-2010.html

Johnson, M. B. (2005). The Central Park Jogger Case– Police Coercion and Secrecy in Interrogation. *Journal of Ethnicity in*

Criminal Justice, 3(1/2), 131-143.

Klarman, M. J. (2009). Scottsboro. *Marquette Law Review, 379*, 379-431. Retrieved from https://dash.harvard.edu/bitstream/handle/1/11226081/Scottsboro.pdf?sequence=2

Kuznar, L. A., Kuznar, E. C., & Aviles, W. (2019). *Inequality, Risk Sensitivity, and Grievance in Context*. Arlington, Virginia: Strategic Multilayer Assessment (SMA) Periodic Publication, OSD/ASD (R&E)/RSD/RRTO.

Majmunder, M. (2017). Higher Rates Of Hate Crimes Are Tied To Income Inequality. Retrieved from https://fivethirtyeight.com/features/higher-rates-of-hate-crimes-are-tied-to-income-inequality/

Saez, E. (2013). Striking it richer: the evolution of top incomes in the United States. *Real-World Economics Review*, (65). Retrieved from https://rwer.wordpress.com/2013/09/27/rwer-issue-65/

Sidky, H. (2018). The War on Science, Anti-Intellectualism, and 'Alternative Ways of Knowing' in 21st-Century America. *Skeptical Inquirer, 42*(2). Retrieved from https://www.csicop.org/si/show/e_war_on_science_anti-intellectualism_and_alternative_ways_of_knowing_in_21

Suedfeld, P., Morrison, B. H., & Kuznar, L. A. (2020). National Interests and the Trump Doctrine: The Meaning of "America First." In S. Renshon & P. Suedfeld (Eds.), *The Trump Doctrine and the Emerging International System*. New York: Palgrave Macmillan.

Vornovitsky, M., Gottschalk, A., & Smith, A. (2011). *Distribution of Household Wealth in the U.S.: 2000 to 2011*. Working Papers of the U.S. Census Bureau, Washington, DC.

Wolff, E. N. (2016). Household Wealth Trends in the United States, 1962 to 2013: What Happened over the Great Recession? *Russell Sage Foundation Journal of the Social Sciences, 2*(6), 24-43.

9. Your Power: Recognizing And Resolving Your Own Paradoxes Of Power

by Joshua M. Hunt and Carl W. Hunt

Asking questions of our nation and our governments, including state and local, is perhaps the single most important act a responsible citizen can take. We are greatly blessed to have the freedom to raise questions and demand answers about how our communities work. Responsible and timely challenges to the representatives we elect are the critical linchpin that separates the free and independent citizens of the United States of America from totalitarianism and dictatorship. This is a special, supremely important power we as American citizens possess and it's also an integral part of our individual power relationships with our community and the organizations of which we might be a part.

This essay is about helping our younger generations in America understand the power of reasonable and appropriate inquiry to frame our representatives' approaches to governing us at the various levels. Good inquiry goes a long way toward helping you recognize and resolve the **Paradoxes of Power** you encounter and helping our nation live up to the potential it can offer to our citizens and to the rest of the world. This essay discusses **Your Power**.

Your second most important power, apart from asking informed questions, is to vote and sensibly select those you would have represent us in government. Voting operationalizes good questions and *wise* voting empowers success at every level. Choosing representatives to govern us does not end on election day, however. Voting and consistently holding the authorities we elect accountable for benefitting the greater good, while protecting the rights of all, are the best ways to empower yourself and avoid paradoxes before they happen.

Ask questions and demand honest answers. Look for organizations to work for and support that strive to improve themselves through good leadership and employee participation. Good leaders will encourage their followers to help everyone do better, whether in government or otherwise. Regardless of the environment, *good leadership is good leadership.* Good leadership may be hard, but so is good followership. To maintain a successful power relationship and avoid paradox in the first place, followers and leaders must all work for each other and their organizations; they must be willing to objectively challenge themselves and each other through meaningful inquiry.

Inquiry: The Power to Discover

Carl's friend and mentor, Dr. David A. Schum, taught him that the questions are often more important than the answers. It is the questions that frame how we perceive our environment and guide our search for answers, although we must be careful to avoid asking questions that bias what we learn and accept as truth or fact. Avoid "confirmation bias," Dave said, explaining how we all too often seek sources and answers that confirm only what we want to know rather than what we need to know. Inquiry and its most valuable tool, the "right" questions, are at the heart of both sound science and good governance. Furthermore, it's those "strategically important questions," as Dave called them, that help us overcome our biases, or at least mitigate them.[97]

Confirmation biases occur when we ask questions or try to interpret their answers in a way that aligns with our personal belief of "how things should be" rather than trying to be objective in our understanding. The thing that makes confirmation bias so problematic is that "being objective" is not natural to the human condition. We experience everything subjectively, personally, so it only makes sense that we should try to interpret new information that way. This process is so natural in fact, that many people do not realize they are subject to biases, which makes it that much more important to understand that they exist and must be addressed as we ask questions.

Since this essay is about "your power," we hope to provide insight on avoiding biases, as well as examples of the types of things we can and should be asking of ourselves, our society, our government, and of leaders at any level of any organization. If you recall from "The Abilene Paradox" example from Chapter 1, a significant organizational shortcoming that led to the group doing something not one of them wanted to do was centered on the fact that none of the members of the group would challenge each other...none of them asked the important questions that would have kept them off the bus. Good inquiry can often keep you off "the bus to Abilene" if you get the questions right.

Let's begin by outlining some strategically important questions for a post-pandemic world (many of which were highly relevant before the pandemic). These questions are only representative of the types all of us should be asking, but particularly our younger generations as they prepare to assume power:

General Organizational Questions and Challenges to Avoid Paradoxes of Power:

- What are the best organizations around that empower us to be active partners and not just passive followers?

- Is the company or organization for which I work willing to invest in *me* and *my development* as I invest in *it* and *its progress towards success*?

- Why do we resist respecting nature, our environment and other living species? Why do we ignore all the signs of climate change and resist building a new economy and living environment that embraces community, sustainability and renewable energy sources that don't harm our environment and other species?

- Why are racism and sexism (or just general inequality) still prevalent in the United States of America? Why aren't these things adequately addressed at a governmental level?

- Why is justice and opportunity greater for some than others? Why does one's level of wealth impact what we as a nation demand as "equal justice under law?"[98]

Specific Questions and Challenges to Elected Representatives and Community:

- Are the political representatives for whom I vote willing to listen to questions that challenge them? Will they address those questions? Will they act on them?

- Why is healthcare so expensive? Why is healthcare tied to employment? Why is it a privilege instead of a right available to all citizens of this nation?

- Why is education so expensive and why are educators underpaid?

- Why does such a large portion of our population look down on science and professionalism?

- Why do we let our leaders pit us against one another when in fact we largely agree on most things as Americans? Why are our politicians seeking to divide us instead of unite us?

- Why do politicians seem to prefer taking care of big business at the expense of small business and local government?

- Why are politicians allowed to seek and take campaign money from businesses and individuals clearly seeking political advantage? Why does the US system of elections need to spend so much money unrelated to anything useful apart from getting elected?

- Why don't Republican and Democratic leaders get along better and agree on more about the one nation to which they took their oath of office?

- What will it take to make the United States of America **United** once again?

We suspect that approaching what have become **Paradoxes of Power** in America with strategically important questions like those posed above, will challenge elected and corporate leaders and hold them to the proper level of accountability. Debate and open inquiry were of great importance during the founding of our nation and the drafting and adoption of our Constitution; it should also be now.

We also believe that asking these questions sets an important example for those in younger generations who have been raised with an emphasis on complacency and an "out of sight out of mind" mentality. If we don't show younger Americans the importance of questioning our leaders and their actions, the proverbial buck may very well stop in the halls of our current dysfunctional Congress and White House. If younger Americans don't begin to challenge the political status quo, politicians will be allowed to continue to further their own agendas with no regard for the good of the country...they may keep leading us down the road on which America's 2016 "leadership" has set us.[99]

Meanwhile, many Americans will grow up oblivious to the inequality problems that permeate our society because they believe they are largely unaffected by them and don't see why they should care. Asking good questions and being receptive to the answers from objective sources, regardless of whether we like them, goes hand in hand with education. This is something Americans of all ages should rediscover for themselves. *Inquiry gives us the power to succeed and ask better questions.*

Operationalizing Your Power

This chapter is not just about asking questions, however. It's also about wisely putting the answers you receive and the discoveries you make to work for the greater good of our families, communities, organizations and indeed to make our nation and our personal futures better.

When we start to ask the kinds of important questions we suggested above, we may quickly find that often, we don't like the answers we receive. Sometimes it is because we don't agree with them, for one reason or another, but other times it is because responses are so unhelpful or rooted in fundamentally flawed logic that they expose the ineptitude or irrationality of those who provide them. When the people offering these less than useful replies occupy positions of leadership or power, it does not take long to lose confidence in their ability, to the point that many people just give up on asking questions because the answers are so frustrating.

This is a power paradox we have discussed multiple times in the essays and Appendix A. This particularly occurs when leaders are elected to positions of power despite their obvious lack of qualifications or knowledge to occupy those positions effectively. We can take things a step further here and extend the paradox to the people who give up on asking the questions yet still expect things to improve. Asking questions is how we expose problems, and if we don't expose the problems, how can we ever expect them to be solved?

This is where **your power** comes in. Every able-minded person on this planet has the power to question things and decide how to react to the answers we get. The second we stop asking questions or decide that answers are "good enough" rather than what we know is consistent and truthful, we allow the ineffective leaders who give us those answers to continue to damage the groups they represent. What's more, you should never be discouraged if your questions elicit outrage or criticism, as this often means *you're asking the right ones.* Just like you, most people don't like to be challenged, especially those in leadership positions. But being held accountable is sometimes the last "check and balance" system we have to separate democracy from dictatorship, regardless of the type of organization. Accountability is a hallmark of good leadership. When you stop asking questions, you forfeit your power in whichever power relationship context you occupy, and you allow someone else's power to continue to let problems go unchecked.

But what if the answers you get are acceptable? What if they seem to be correct? Does this mean you can stop inquiring about things and just go about your business? Unfortunately, the answer may be no. Accepting things as absolute fact, regardless of how "correct" you perceive them to be, is how you fall into the "out of sight out of mind" paradox. It is easy to believe that if you are personally happy with responses to your inquiries, that must mean that everything is fine. In reality, it may mean you need to start asking different questions, particularly if the problems you first uncovered keep happening and scale up to affect others. It means you need to use your power for the greater good; you need to think about people other than yourself and ask the kinds of questions that might benefit them, too.

So now that we've asked all these questions, what exactly do we do with the answers we get? This is where the next step in making the most of **your** power manifests. In chapter 4, Marc Hill included an incredibly inspiring quote from the late American politician John Lewis, who believed that if a person sees something wrong, that person should take action to fix it. In fact, the original quote from Congressman Lewis appears at the front of this book. Applying Marc's recounting of this excellent logic to our current conversation, if you receive an answer that you find unacceptable, or that you know is morally suspect, it is your duty to act on it.

This is usually the point where you start to hear people say things like:

"Oh, well my voice doesn't matter, so I'll just keep my opinions to myself."

"How is someone like me going to make any change…why even try?"

"It's just easier to forget about it and move on. What can "little old me" do, anyway?"

These are excuses and self-justifications. They are ways of thinking through challenges in which we try to rationalize in-action and defend the squandering of our personal power because doing nothing feels like the easy way out. But who ever said that having power would be easy? Trying to affect change *is not easy.* This is exactly the reason our country has so many problems—most people opt for the easy way out and choose not to act rather than to try and help solve things.

When you hear an answer to an important question that is unsatisfactory or that you know is wrong, *take it and run with it.* Run to your friends to explain the problem you see. Run to your computer to write in a blog or send something to a local news source or your local representative's office. Run to your city council, or to any other forum you can find where you can share what's bothering you. For every person who decides to use their personal power in this way, one more voice gets heard. And when enough voices get heard, change starts to happen. It can be a frustratingly slow process, to be sure, but the more that people speak up the faster it eventually goes, and even five miles per hour is faster than zero, which is how quickly things move when one does nothing.

In conclusion, *ask questions about your leaders' actions.* Government leaders, business leaders, religious leaders, it doesn't matter. All leaders who wield power should be subject to their followers' inquiries—it's their duty! This is how we as followers use our personal power to help maintain balance in the relationship. And when we get useful answers, *act on them.* Both good answers and bad answers should be shared in as many ways as possible, so that the former can be praised and carried forward as examples and the latter can be questioned even further and brought to peoples' attention, and we can jointly participate in corrective action.

Failing to do these things lands us in our own little personal **Paradoxes of Power**, where inaction seems favorable and looking for the easy way out becomes a way of life. Meanwhile, we become more and more hypocritical, complaining about the state of the things we refused to try and fix. "Out of sight, out of mind" and "the path of least resistance" are the two main ways we let leaders get away with abuses and misuses of power that have influenced the American way of life for far too long.

Take control of your personal power and stand up for what is right. Let's get the United States of America **United** *once again.*

10. The Future Of Power

by The Editorial Team

-Joshua M. Hunt, Carl W. Hunt, and Our Esteemed Essayists

When we began to plan the writing for Chapter 10 (and Chapter 11), we quickly realized that an essay on the Future of Power required input from the entire essay team. We framed five basic categories of inquiry to guide the preparation of the Chapters, keying on the ways in which we might see the evolution of power in the United States and the West unfold. Within the responses we also found clues to how power in the rest of world might also play out as we moved forward into a rapidly changing climate and social environment. What follows is speculation, of course, but speculation informed by experience, education and a willingness to take risks in predicting our future as both a nation and indeed as a species. Perhaps the risks the Founders faced in 1787 are also an inspiration for success in the risks we think America faces in 2020 and beyond.

In essence, we gathered all of our essayists (virtually, of course) to comment on the future of political power, racial and gender power and progress, the essence of power as it relates to Mother Nature, how the COVID-19 pandemic affects us now and in the future, and the future narrative America must have for its citizens and the rest of the world (as it relates to power relationships, both individually and collectively). We began to posit a beginning of what we called the "pre-post history" of power in national and international relationships.

One important thing we concluded was that as the future of our democratic experiment unfolds, the people of our nation need up-

dated narratives about ourselves and our fellow Americans; the effective application of power is at the center of this need. We address that at the end of this essay.

The "Strategically Important Questions"

What follows are the abridged versions of some of the most important framing questions we used, some more provocative than others, and a recap of the responses we received from the editorial team composed of the essayists in the book. We sought to expand thinking "out of the box" rather than constrain it. Interestingly, the idea of a new American narrative, discussed at the conclusion of this chapter, surfaced as a response in multiple questions. These questions follow:[100]

1. What would you think of a "Constitutional Convention of 2022" that might address our lessons learned as a nation since the first convention of 1787? It could update our thoughts and policies on modern commerce, international relationships, elections, global affairs, as well as reexamine other conditions and provisions that simply don't exist any longer. We might also address technology-enabled communications, air and space travel, climate change and advanced science and research investment. We use this "metaphor" of a constitutional convention to suggest the serious nature of change that our nation might require to pull away from the divisiveness that has pervaded our politics and society for the last 50 years or so.

2. The multiple challenges our nation has in embracing equality of treatment of women and minority Americans continues, as Chapters 3 and 4 vividly discuss.[101] Why does America refuse to fully accept that "all men are created equal" which of course means *all people*? What are the appropriate actions we must take to ensure that everyone does indeed have the same access to opportunity and the freedoms our Constitution, as amended, ultimately guarantees?

3. Chapter 6, "Human Power versus Nature's Power," and follow-on blog posts such as Josh's "Your vote in 2020 may literally save the planet" from August 13, 2020, and Carl's and CE Hunt's Nature and Man: The "Ultimate" Paradox of Power, from August 28, 2020, have strongly emphasized the paradoxical conflicts humanity has chosen to pursue against nature. We propose that until recently (the last 25 years or so), based on Stuart Kauffman's (and others) work, most people didn't understand what we were doing to the world which nurtures and sustains us. Since the dawn of 2000, however, there have been no mysteries about the impact of climate change except those we choose to disregard. What actions, including better marketing strategies, might we employ to help Americans retake the global leadership role in climate protection and change mitigation? How might our economy change, perhaps improve, as a result?

4. The COVID-19 Pandemic has deeply impacted our society and economy in ways that will reverberate for years to come. Aside from the loss of human life caused directly by the virus, some of the greatest concerns moving forward are how our country can recover from the historic unemployment rates it currently faces, as well as the deeply troubling economic news we've all been experiencing since the pandemic began. Many companies are staring down the barrel of having to close their businesses as consumers are forced to shift from shopping in person to shopping online or just not buying non-essential things at all. What do you think the government should be doing, if anything, to support the American people affected by COVID-related job loss or business closure? Does the concept of **Paradoxes of Power** apply to such economic solutions?

5. Do Americans need a new narrative?[102] If so, and we propose we do, how could it be shaped so that more Americans can buy into it? What is the correct tone for such a narrative?

How would a new narrative succeed over the long term when so many previous attempts have failed to live up to their potential to change America and unite us on a more permanent basis...what would make a new narrative different? What are the mechanisms we need in place to build new narrative to avoid future **Paradoxes of Power**?

What follows are a series of amalgamated responses formed from the feedback we got from our various writers and contributors in their considerations of these questions. Those responses not attributed directly to their authors should be attributed to Joshua and Carl.

Responses and Implications for the Future of Power

1. The "Constitutional Convention of 2022"

Generally, the essayists support the notion of a new Constitutional Convention. Admittedly however, any enthusiasm is tempered by a realistic assessment that the United States is likely far too divided to take on this kind of mission, at least as things stand today. To make this happen, we must find areas of common ground, as well as the compelling need, to rewrite or significantly amend our Constitution. Somehow, we managed to find just enough need and common ground in 1787, although the compromises we made as an early nation still divide us now. Despite such a necessary precondition of having a strong majority of people in this country "on the same page," we are cautiously optimistic that enough people will come to understand the need for change in the not-too-distant future.

As essayist Lawrence (Larry) Kuznar wrote, "I support the concept, but I fear that we are too divided to pull this off at the moment. I know the original constitutional convention was contentious and many times was on the brink of collapse. Moreover, the Founders were influenced by a foundation of enlightenment ideals like rationality and compromise that I fear we have all but destroyed. We need to be sure that we have rebuilt that foundation before this could be attempted. This book hopefully will be a step in that direction, but the trail is long."

Dennis Greene added, "Based on our current state of affairs, this nation will need much, much more than a Constitutional Convention to repair the carnage of this current administration. How do we bring back many tens of thousands of COVID-19 lives lost due to the inactions of this administration? How do we rejoin children seeking amnesty with their families, many left to dwell in cages for months on end? How do we counter an administration leveraging anarchy as a political strategy? Arnold Schwarzenegger, former Republican California governor said today, August 30, 2020, on national television, 'The time for dialogue is over. The time for action is now.' So okay, let's do the 2022 Constitutional Convention as part of a larger effort to save our democracy. Let's do something because our house, our USA, is nearing autocratic rule."

Veronica Mata posed an interesting perspective, "I like to think of this challenge like I would a business. The most successful businesses evolve, they grow, they develop, and they change. Their policies, employee handbooks, regulations, and expectations change, so why shouldn't our country? A company, like JP Morgan Chase which was founded in 1799, 77 years before the telephone was invented, isn't going to operate today without telephones 'just because that's what the founders did, and we should too.' If the companies within our country are constantly 'removing onerous provisions' and addressing more current topics, why shouldn't our government? Look how far we've come over 245 years, and how much we still must change."

CE Hunt concluded, "we all hope people will come to realize that our current Constitution systematically ensures that rules for the many are made by a very select few. In a perfect democracy, the 'few' would understand the needs of the 'many,' and would make their decisions accordingly in a way that would do the most good for the most people (considering and respecting minority rights, of course).

"Unfortunately, this perfect scenario is a far cry from the way things work today and the current way is unsustainable. As an example of a Constitutional reform we might suggest, let's look at the US Senate. In an updated Constitution, perhaps each state would be ensured one seat, but the rest would be allocated by population, not unlike the House. We might limit this new Senate, however, to somewhere around 150 people.[103] To put the importance of this change into perspective, is it really right or fair that Wyoming receives more clout in the Senate than California or Texas purely on a per capita basis? We question that feature of Section 3 of Article 1 in 2020."

CE's question about the Senate is worth considering. The composition of the Senate, particularly as practiced in recent years, facilitates deadlock by very conservative, lesser populated states in the Western US, even if there was a substantial liberal majority in the rest of the Senate. This applies the other way around, as well, when Democrats might hold up legislation in a Republican majority, as seen in recent years. As long as the filibuster and 60-vote rules to invoke cloture are frequently used in today's Senate, the potential for deadlock threatens productive action, thus ensuring a **Paradox of Power** in governmental leadership and legislation. We've seen these paradoxes surface during attempts to provide COVID-19 relief, for example. Perhaps Senate composition and administration could be altered by a new Constitution or even Constitutional Amendment, but we also recognize it's particularly challenging to change a system that was designed to ensure a more deliberative legislative body in a bicameral structure that has worked reasonably well, most of the time, for so many years...until recently.

Another area we see that is ripe for reform is the electoral college (as described in Title 3 of the US Code). The way it works today is archaic and problematic in America's modernized and diverse society. It should not be possible that a potential president can lose a popular vote but still ascend to power, because it literally *defies the logic and reason behind democracy.* There is no reason that voting for a president (or any other position of power) should be any more complicated than counting peoples' votes and seeing who got the majority—the most pure and fundamental form of people choosing their leader. What's more, the current setup that for the most part involves "winner-take-all" state selection of presidential electors completely skews the concept of fair and equal representation. Candidates are encouraged to focus more on some states and demographics while completely ignoring others because of the perception that those states don't matter to the success of the campaign.

It's no wonder that some people believe their votes don't matter when we have politicians who believe in such "pragmatism" as campaign where it counts...to them. Finally, the way things are done now creates a very real scenario where third-party candidates can significantly alter the outcome of an election by throwing off the numbers in only a few certain states. In a system where each person's vote counts as one vote and that's the end of it, this effect is greatly mitigated if not eliminated completely. We count all the votes and whoever gets the most votes is the winner.

On the face of it, the Founders rejected the idea of a popular vote to elect the president for reasons that were likely justified at the time. They were influenced by a foundation of enlightenment ideals like rationality and compromise that have been all but destroyed over the last few decades. If we were ever to attempt any changes to the electoral college, we should surely have to rebuild that foundation of reason if we hope to succeed and avoid future paradoxes. At a minimum, we could empower and encourage states to ensure that electors represent all the voters, not just the ones who happened to vote for the candidate who received the most ballots in the state, as winner-take-all laws do now.[104]

Addressing science and technology issues, particularly climate change, would be an absolute necessity at the new convention. The current Constitution gives us Clause 8 of Section 8 of Article I (Federal Legislative Bodies) which does address the "Progress of Science and useful Arts" in terms of patent protections, but it's not much; it is far from comprehensive in its application to the types of science and technology advances we as a nation have experienced since 1787. We suspect a new convention would take the time to thoroughly lay out contemporary approaches that meet the needs of our modern and ever-evolving world. The same likely applies to innovative forms of transportation, trade and global relationships, and many other issues that are far more complex today than at the founding of our nation.

It is unlikely that a new or amended Constitution would solve all our present problems, but if it was drafted and designed by the right group of people it could improve the outlook of our country significantly. As far as what that "right group of people" looks like, we would suggest that they need to be intelligent, objective thinkers who are free from prejudice and genuinely interested in the needs of our country, its people, and our planet. The convention would not be composed of a body of white males, as it was in 1787, but would be fully representative of our population. It would also need to possess an understanding of the malfunctions in power relationships that have emerged since 1787 to avoid the creation of new power paradoxes.

2. Power relationships related to gender and minority challenges in the United States

This question was challenging to address. Most of the authors of this book have never and will never directly experience the prejudices and persecution faced by women and people of color in this country. Thankfully, we were fortunate to be joined by some truly remarkable people who provided that perspective and helped us to understand things better.

"Nations love legacies and traditions," Veronica Mata wrote. "Fear, social norms (that have been in place for generations, specifically in this country), and those who made it to positions of power grooming their successors to think and act like them, contribute greatly to the disconnects between gender and race. The **Paradox of Power**, specifically with women and minorities, is that we forget power is not mutually exclusive of leadership. Essentially, people who informally wield power (e.g., are not in 'formal' leadership positions) forget that they still need to be leaders, and that leadership is more than just telling people what to do or being the face of a group of people, and even more than fighting for that group of people. Leadership is about inspiring others, working with others, and teaching others how to be leaders themselves. On the other side of this coin, though, those with privilege need to start recognizing their responsibility to call out the others who also have privilege and are taking it for granted, abusing it, or not using it in a productive way. They need to recognize their roles in creating paradoxes."

Also, as Dennis Greene noted, "America does accept equality for the most part, however, it's based on a White American paradoxical notion that we're all on a mostly colorblind, somewhat level playing field. In other words, many in White America believe in equality on their terms; this is not necessarily the full truth. This explains the crux of this power paradox. Although helpful, no amount of policies and laws will significantly change hearts and minds, much like Southern White indifference following the signing of the Civil Rights Act of 1964, capped by the murder of Dr. Martin Luther King in 1968. Yes, the law changed for the better, and that is a good thing, but this country must pursue truth and reconciliation, akin to South Africa following Apartheid, to begin facilitating the permanent change we seek, moving from chaos to community. We must begin to do this now."

The consensus of the essayists is that as a nation, "we've been here before." We have raised awareness and promoted change, only to see people fall back into the same divided mindsets for one reason or another. For many people, the problem is not a hard stance against women or minorities. The problem is an apathetic or unmotivated way of thinking that is based on the perception that "things that don't affect me don't matter." In chapters 4 and 9, we referred to this as the "out of sight out of mind" mentality. This phenomenon can be observed across many demographics, but young-to-middle-aged white males seem to be affected at a disproportionately higher rate, particularly when it comes to a lack of sensitivity to racial inequality issues. More perplexing is that so many whites, male and female, have allowed themselves to fall into the victim trap, embracing fear of non-whites, instead of hope for America's more diverse future.[105]

On the other hand, it is impossible to ignore the number of blatantly racist Americans who have emerged from behind their facades of acceptance and tolerance, emboldened by some of the sentiments of the current presidential administration. Fortunately, movements like Black Lives Matter have risen to the challenge of combatting this negativity with the inspiration of love and acceptance. It is tragic that this call to action must come at the cost of the lives of countless victims of police brutality and violence, but it would be far more tragic for their sacrifices to have been in vain. This cause has brought people of all races together in a way that was previously unknown to younger generations of Americans, and in that there is reason for hope.

When we add gender into the equation, we see a different problem at the root of the inequality. The idea that men should be strong, and that power comes from physical strength, has existed since the earliest humans started living in groups together. The sentiment only gained momentum as certain civilizations began to develop faster and conquer others, adding the perception that the "people in power" should look, speak, or act a certain way; this began to blur the lines between gender inequality and race inequality. Before we knew it, we had an environment where "western civilization" was put on a pedestal (by Westerners) and being a white male was, by proxy, the most powerful default position in which one could find oneself.

We believe the cumulative effect of all of this is that many, if not all the inequality problems we face today are rooted in white males' fear of losing their masculinity, status, or associated identity. This is by no means a blanket statement that assumes that all Caucasian men must act or feel this way, but an attempt to identify a prominent underlying causality to accompany our observations. Fear is hardly the answer, because no truer words were ever spoken than FDR's "the only thing we have to fear is fear itself."[106]

Is there a solution for a more positive future of all-people power? We suggest *humility*. Humility is a fundamental aspect of acceptance, both of our own circumstances and those of others around us. It is also an important part of empathy, and a quality that tempers fear, envy and hatred. For many people, humility is hard to teach and even harder to learn, but it must become a focus for current and future generations. Education in general must become more of a focus, but emotional education and maturity must play just as big a role as studies such as history, math, or science if we are to improve as both humans and thinkers.

Another solution? Continue to question and challenge the people who lead us and the world we build...be appropriately skeptical. Resist the temptation to accept reality because it happens to suit you today. There are others who are not in the same position because of circumstances beyond their control such as race or gender and their reality may be far less acceptable. Americans must recognize that the human quest for equality is one whose outcome will benefit everyone, even if they can't specifically see how it benefits them at that point in time. With equality comes balance: balance of power in leadership, and a more well-balanced society where opportunities are available to all. This is how we maximize *the sum of our parts;* this is how we avoid **Paradoxes of Power**. The responses to Question 5 on the new American Narrative, below, fit well into resolving the future of power in equality for gender and race.

3. Human Power versus Nature's Power

"Probably more than anything else, the US needs a functional legislative capability that can act even when there is political disagreement—inaction due simply to political differences is unacceptable and does our nation no good whatsoever," notes CE Hunt. For reasons that may defy common sense, a very significant portion of our population keeps returning politicians to office that are committed to the status quo of maintaining legacy energy production even though that production has been *proven to close down future options.*

Our nation's politically driven assessments of energy generation, including legacy subsidies and removal of pollution controls and devices by the current administration (as of September, 2020), are unneeded and counterproductive...they ignore the immense business opportunities for international leadership in new forms of energy production. Simply put, there is not a single long-term case for maintaining "business as usual" in energy production and consumption, while there is a significant case to transition to renewable energy sources soon.

As Dennis Greene notes, "The effects of climate change are self-evident to us and to most of the world. Change will happen congruently with the economic benefits of reducing our carbon footprint. For instance, when solar and wind produce electricity more efficiently than fossil fuels, then those solutions will prevail. Technology is our national linchpin. Let's use it to the fullest extent, for example, perfecting fuel cell technology, collectively with other power levers such as policy and social education, to save our planet for all future generations."

So, how do we do this? Larry Kuznar proposes that "we find a way to make people care." *But how do we do that?* CE Hunt notes "this is going to be the biggest challenge any progressive new incoming politicians will face for years to come. Climate change is another area where Americans so readily settle into the 'out of sight out of mind' mentality." Of course, this statement doesn't assume to represent everyone. There are plenty of environmental heroes and champions out there fighting the good fight, but it seems logical to assume that if these earth-conscious folks represented the majority, we wouldn't be in the situation we're in now, with irreversible damage to the environment breathing down our necks.

Larry continues, "although it might sound somewhat inane, we need to find a way to make confronting climate change *sexy*. After all, nothing motivates Americans to do something like the perception that the admiration or desire of others will reward an action. Maybe if we could find a way to associate doing good things for the environment with being held in high esteem, more people would be likely to take part. But then we'd have to get the message out there somehow."

Veronica Mata is onboard with this line of thinking, too. "The trigger word is marketing. Money, for example, is always a great incentive. People don't realize when you save water, you're really saving money. Recycling is trickier in the sense it's harder to monetize the value, but one thing I really loved about living in California was that they had recycling stations where anyone from a middle class family member, to a lower income family member, to even a homeless person (and there were many environmentally conscious homeless in California), can go and recycle their bottles and cans at this unit and get money back (it was like a big ATM, almost). Now it wasn't a lot per item, maybe 10-20 cents, but for a lot of people that adds up. Education in all levels of schools must be a focus. I didn't start seeing recycling and compost bins around campus until college (I went to middle school and high school in Colorado). Maybe the bottom line is that there is so much involved with climate change that it needs to be broken down for people. What can we really do today...tomorrow...next month? What really makes a difference? Many people can't walk or bike to work or don't have the time to take public transportation, so what else can they do? What can we do as individuals and as a unified nation to be better recyclers? This needs to be shared knowledge and marketed so that it just becomes common sense."

In our modern era of connectivity, some of this responsibility falls directly to those with social media "reach" (see also: "clout"). If actors, athletes, and more importantly other forms of "influencers" committed to the spread of this message, *the message would spread,* and it would spread like wildfire. If anyone can make something "sexy" these days, it's social media personalities. These people also have access to just about every demographic, and more importantly, they have access to younger Americans, with whom it has become more difficult to connect over the years through the more traditional means of social engagement.

Larry further points out that "environmental awareness doesn't just need to be attractive though; it specifically needs to be attractive to the people in younger generations who have the chance to make the most change moving forward. Energy is central to peoples' lives, and it has been since its discovery.[107] Americans consume 17% of the world's energy according to the U.S. government,[108] but make up only 4% of the world's population. This is clearly unbalanced and unsustainable; and similarly to equality, education about it needs to start young and stay strong throughout the development of our youths and young adults if we are to overcome the standard of stigma and ignorance the GOP-led side of the government has tried to set for caring about the earth."

This environmental movement will need new voices, but not all of them should come from younger Americans. We will need older generations to get on board too, and to acknowledge that the consequences of our previous inaction will likely be in effect before this becomes "somebody else's problem." Make no mistake, if you currently live on this planet, climate change is *your problem*. If you have lived on this planet for decades, climate change *was* your problem, and now it *still is*. We need people of every age to accept that the trade-off we made for getting to live in such a developed country and society is the responsibility to try to counteract the damage we did to the planet to get here.

If there was any one place in this book that the phrase "we're all in this together" applied, this would be it. Overcoming our **Paradox of Power** with nature is a quest that transcends all others in existence, because *existence* won't continue if we destroy the world on which we *exist*. The future of power related to almost everything human requires us to take care of the world of which we are a part and not above, as Chapter 6 discusses.

4. Economic Power

The COVID-19 pandemic has clearly challenged the ways in which we think about and execute our local and national economies. Many small businesses, categorically one of the leading employers in America, have had to find new ways to cope, but mostly through concerned communities that supported necessary changes in their business models (e.g., take out or delivery). Small businesses are typically service-sector companies and thus rely heavily on their local base of customers. Larger businesses often rely on supplying smaller organizations and thus they are interdependent on locally owned small business customer bases as well, even if recognition of that important fact falls short.

The importance of small business and their customer bases

also point to another phenomenon that Larry Kuznar discussed at the beginning of Chapter 5, Power and Paradox in the Post Pandemic Economy: the notion of "complexity economics," formally introduced by Brian Arthur in 2013. Arthur discussed three broad themes about modern economies, all of which apply in the post-pandemic world, but it is his third theme we will discuss here (the first two dealt with dynamism and constant novelty). That third need is for inductive reasoning to understand how hard it is to predict "real-world economies."

Inductive thinking, in philosophical terms, means to reason from smaller to larger domains...from the bottom up...rather than the top down. This also means thinking in terms of emergence that arises from complex system interactions.[109] That's exactly what we're facing in trying to visualize the future of power when it comes to economics. There's more uncertainty in reasoning about future economic power, but it's a worthwhile consideration since it affects all of us in this nation and drives so much of political power as well.

The essayists' perspectives varied in their responses to questions of the future of economic power. Dennis Greene pointed out that "over 40 million Americans have been processed for unemployment, as of this writing, now averaging over a million weekly claims. As Executive Director of our local Chamber of Commerce (Greenwood Village, CO, and The Denver Technology Center), I have seen the effects of job and opportunity loss, leading to personal loss on many levels. There is no silver bullet solution, however innovation to repurpose our national labor pool must happen now. So how does this happen? I say we look back to FDR's Works Progress Administration (WPA) model, combined with a national GI Education Bill and student loan forgiveness for displaced Americans. The benefits to our nation will greatly outweigh any argument posed by the anti-tax crowd, all of whom pulled a Houdini and disappeared in recent years to spend on their personal and political agendas. However, we should look to mitigate costs by reversing the recent GOP income tax amendments and yes, have corporations pay their 'fair share' for the right (and privilege) to operate in this great nation."

Veronica Mata represents small business directly...two of them as a matter of fact. As an entrepreneur and business founder, Veronica has direct experience in seeking government assistance that was targeted to help small business. "My biggest complaint in the recent governmental support has been regarding small business aid. I officially hate the Small Business Association. Sure, our small business benefited, but 1.) Not nearly as much as the 'small businesses' that were on that list (e.g., Kayne West's company, Yeezy, and indirectly, Jared Kushner's family holdings, were reported to benefit)[110], and 2.) it was only enough to cover one month's rent (when we had to close for two months, and have been deeply affected for the past seven months). My beef with the SBA is how they classify small businesses: '500 employees or less.' 500! That's not a small business that's a middle-level to corporate-level business. Certainly, that's a lot of jobs on the line, but for many small business owners, (and their employees) that one truly small business is their only source of income. Small business owners already take on a lot of financial responsibility, not only in running the business, but they rarely have a pension, paid time off, health benefits, nor can they afford to fund workmen's compensation. These are extra financial challenges that need to be addressed in any small business assistance. True small businesses are run by people who are in the business, working the day-to-day operations. They're the ones in the trenches."

Some of the essayists thought we'd see an eventual resurgence of economic power exercised on the part of consumers and small businesses, while others believed that big companies would only get bigger. Given the pace of unemployment, which seems to be borne more by small companies and the rates in which they have been shuttered during the pandemic, the idea is valid that big companies would exploit opportunities to fill the gaps left by the loss of local, small business.[111] While there have been several notable larger companies declaring bankruptcy during the pandemic, there is debate about those companies' viability even before COVID-19 struck the US, so those losses may not be relevant to the future of small business.

Other essayists believed that post-pandemic economies will ultimately place more of the "power" of the consumer in the hands of small businesses and those they serve. Increasingly, larger companies will no longer be "in charge" of what goods or services we buy if they want to stay in the traditional business of supplying smaller businesses. While it may not have started that way at the beginning of our nation, the shift towards supply-side economics, perhaps great for production efficiencies, was a **Paradox of Power** in that supply-and-demand was strongly skewed to the supply world. Manufacturing and modern supply chains may have developed great cost-savings from centralized production and distribution, but they may have also contributed to significant resource waste and greater energy consumption. Producing a lot of widgets at a lower price if those widgets simply end up in a garbage dump is hardly efficient.

In truth, we must wait to see how things play out, but there is reason to hope that there will be room for win-wins that ultimately benefit consumers in ways that allow a more level playing field between large and small companies. In the meantime, there have been indicators over the last few decades that support the shifting of economic power to less centralized methods. If there is a power shift, it's likely that the supply-and-demand model will not change dramatically except that the demand will be more consumer driven than supply driven. That means the bottom-up economy will ultimately "control more of the action" and more power will shift to the bottom, as it were. It seems reasonable that consumer demands are met rather than supplier demands anyway. We see the potential for such a shift taking place in the near future, as predicted at least as far back as Alvin and Heidi Toffler's thinking in books like *Future Shock*, *The Third Wave* and *Power Shift*.[112]

Such shifts could have enduring and significant consequences on manufacturing and transportation, as well, emphasizing local production over centralized production. Large warehouse-based supply businesses, such as Amazon and Walmart, will likely continue to have a major role to play as cost-effective home delivery will still be important for a time, but even that may shift to more localized delivery services to capitalize on "just-in-time" manufacturing as these capabilities grow in even greater popularity. Over time, it may make far less sense to have huge power-hungry footprints for warehouses just to produce and store "stuff" until it's needed, an unsustainable economic model that is a hold-over from economy-of-scale platforms of the past.

The consequences for production, transportation, power generation and consumption may soon be driven more by local demand than global demand, and that could be a good thing for our environment and our living spaces if that were to come pass. That would necessarily change the way Americans look at consumption, of course, as we scale back our desires to be more consistent with our needs. If we could do that, we could create far more localized, environmentally friendly production and delivery systems that bring us together in community rather than split us apart. We could see a "power shift" back to a more local perspective as Americans rethink consumption. The final section of this chapter, A New American Narrative, looks at a 10-year old prescriptive essay that begins to discuss this especially important concept, as does a paper produced by two of our essayists a few years ago.[113]

If these kinds of changes do take place, economic power clearly swings from national-to-local relationships and would be far more sensitive to local needs rather than national requirements that maintain a focus primarily on supply. It seems that the local world is exactly where the power should be to be most sensitive to what's really needed as opposed to what some marketing-advertising campaign tells consumers they should want. That's a model of economic power located where it should be: in the hands of the consumers.

5. A New American Narrative

At the beginning of this chapter, we referred to what we called a "pre-post history" of power in national and international relationships. If such a thing existed, this would describe prognostications on what our history would explain about America at some point in the future after we've gotten past the current divisiveness and malfunctions of power, known as the "Trump era."[114] This final section on the Future of Power is an attempt to depict what we badly need in our nation: a new narrative about who we are and what we want to become.

One thing that has surfaced from the "Trump era" in the recent political campaigns of both parties is a discussion on fear versus hope. Any new narrative we select for ourselves as Americans must be based on hope, just as the Founders were focused in 1787. We must be able to convince ourselves, which would in turn help to convince the rest of the world, that America is built on optimism and not on a fearfulness that paralyzes us into inaction, disengagement and even more anxiety. We must visualize and work towards the future our Founders hoped their experiment would eventually produce.

For this reason, we close this chapter and indeed our book with a look to a hopeful vision of America based on the work in which one of Carl's friends participated about ten years ago. This friend, Dr. Wayne Porter (Captain, US Navy retired), and a colleague, Colonel Mark Mykleby (United States Marine Corps, retired), prepared a study for their boss for whom they both worked directly in the Pentagon. Their boss was Admiral Mike Mullen (US Navy, retired) who was then the Chairman of the Joint Chiefs of Staff. Their study project was known as "A National Strategic Narrative" and it captured a great deal of national and international attention in the years right after its public release in 2011.[115]

Several key points about this narrative make it highly relevant to our discussions about the future of power in America. The first is that American power must be based on "the core values and principles enshrined in our Constitution and proven through war and peace," as the authors noted. These values produce our national character, and without these values, "America has no credibility." We've seen elsewhere in our essays that these values are under siege over the last 50 years, particularly when they are misused to produce the **Paradoxes of Power** we've described throughout.

Porter and Mykleby characterized these values as follows:

(they are) reflected in a wider global application: tolerance for all cultures, races, and religions; global opportunity for self-fulfillment; human dignity and freedom from exploitation; justice with compassion and equality under internationally recognized rule of law; sovereignty without tyranny, with assured freedom of expression; and an environment for entrepreneurial freedom and global prosperity, with access to markets, plentiful water and arable soil, clean and abundant energy, and adequate health services.[116]

If we begin to emphasize these values as guiding principles by which to apply sound leadership principles we've described throughout the book, we will take a huge step forward in mitigating and resolving the paradoxes our essayists have documented in their works.

But, there's more that can guide us and cement the directions we need to take as we build the future of power in the United States. Porter and Mykleby describe two anchors of American strength: *prosperity* and *security*; these are "our enduring national interests." Both pillars of American success do and must continue to interact with each other, based on our values, to produce our power. Our national power, and indeed all the individual powers and rights we enjoy, stem from the linkages of American prosperity and security. They depend on each other and we need the strength of their mutual interdependencies and interactions.

And we're not done yet if we want to benefit from a new narrative for America. We also need to invest. Porter and Mykleby write that our nation needs to focus on three investment priorities. The first is our young people, the very object of our book, **Paradoxes of Power**. We are gratified that "A National Strategic Narrative" recognizes the critical need to build the "intellectual capital and a sustainable infrastructure of education, health and social services to provide for the continuing development and growth of America's youth." The second investment priority the authors call out is a sustainable "whole of nation" security that includes all aspects of being a member of the American society and culture, not just national defense as it relates to military power. Finally, "our third investment priority is to develop a plan for the sustainable access to, cultivation and use of, the natural resources we need for our continued wellbeing, prosperity and economic growth in the world marketplace," Porter and Mykleby write. And as we know from Chapter 6, this investment priority may only be achieved when we avoid the paradoxes we described between humans and nature.

While there are several other relevant topics in this "new narrative" for America, we mention the capstone recommendation for what the authors call a *Strategic Ecosystem*: "A National Prosperity and Security Act." In 1947, President Harry Truman signed into law the National Security Act of 1947, and it remains today a guide for national security in our nation. Porter and Mykleby describe the next generation of such a potentially long-enduring measure, and it combines the strength of the 1947 law with an additional emphasis on enhancing prosperity for our nation, as they described in "our enduring national interests," above. This act would "recognize the need to take a longer view, a generational view, for the sustainability of our nation's security and prosperity."

As Porter and Mykleby define this new approach to American governance, this National Prosperity and Security Act:

would integrate policy across agencies and departments of the Federal government and provide for more effective public/private partnerships; increase the capacity of appropriate government departments and agencies; align Federal policies, taxation, research and development expenditures and regulations to coincide with the goals of sustainability; and, converge domestic and foreign policies toward a common purpose." That, when combined with updated state and local government policies, is how we build the base for the future of power in our nation.[117]

In summary, we already have a comprehensive model to generate a new narrative for America that harnesses all the creativity and original objectivity our Founders intended. Even if some of the main areas of social interaction between men and women, whites and non-whites, property-owning and non-property owning Americans got off to a rough start at the writing and ratification or our Constitution, many of the basic provisions endure, and in fact, empower us for our future. The Founders provided us with not only a Constitution, they also provided us with the underpinnings of our national narrative. Now we can run with that, integrate the vision of important past works such as Porter's and Mykleby's, and produce a narrative that fits America in 2020. This is the basis of our future power of America.

And as our readers might expect, we don't see success in simply considering just one or two of these areas of inquiry as the underpinning of the future of power in America. No, we think that all these areas must be studied and integrated, along with other areas that will emerge while we consider the five questions we pose above. Interaction and integration, combined with the power of emergence and richness of complexity, will produce a future of power that is less subject to the fragility that paradox introduces and more meaningful to America.

While we can introduce the makings of a **Paradox of Power** with just one or two abuses, it takes a lot of "effort" to produce the kind of widespread and divisive power relationship abuses we've examined throughout the book. We've been at this power malfunction for quite a while. Unfortunately, paradoxes have a cascading effect that make them difficult to stop, and we must keep this mind while designing ways to mitigate and overcome paradoxes. The five areas we mention in this chapter, the basis for futures of power, are elementary and essential starting points to be sure. They must be designed in ways that allow them to interact and coevolve successfully. This coevolutionary process will produce emergences, as we've discussed throughout the book. Addressing the five areas of inquiry honestly, no matter how uncomfortable they may be for America today, will be the key to how the future of power in our nation unfolds.

11. Epilogue

by Joshua and Carl

We've come a long way since first proposing the existence of **Paradoxes of Power** and how they cause significant disruptions to leadership, followership and success in America. In fact, they affect power relationships throughout the world. In the course of proposing that these misuses and abuses of power can be identified, studied and resolved, we've examined instances of paradoxes in the context of gender, race, economics, nature, government, education, justice and even religion. We've demonstrated the pervasive nature of power relationships and how they malfunction all too often in practically every category of life.

Our study and the insights we gained from our essayists revealed paradoxes that we rarely considered before. For example, in the area of human power versus nature's power, why would we even want to resist all that nature has done to nurture us just so we can make a little more money, produce a little more energy or create a new version of a widget that wasn't even that useful in the first place? To us on the essay team, that's totally paradoxical. In terms of economic power, what use do we have for the accumulation of billions of dollars in wealth while others around us live in poverty...how big a house do we need...how big a car do we really require? That's paradoxical, as well. Why do some of us insist that our religious beliefs are so "pure" that anyone else's beliefs can only lead to damnation. Isn't that paradoxical, also?

In what is another **Paradox of Power** that affects every American directly is the apparent way in which roughly half of us have chosen *fear* over *hope*. Our Founders took a realistic perspective in drafting the Constitution in 1787; they also held out optimism not only in the outcomes of their debates in launching a new kind of democratic experiment, but also in the future of an already diverse population of people. Even the newest Americans of 1776 came from varying backgrounds, classes and professions. Very few of them understood what it could mean to live in a nation where potentially everyone was free to think the way they desired, could own property and ultimately select their own leaders—that was not characteristic of any other contemporary government. For the most part, they all had a sense of hope that outweighed the fears they also experienced.

Because this is an election season, moving from the publication of this book in September 2020 into the elections of November 2020, we used political and governance examples of power paradoxes to illustrate the damage that malfunctioning political power brings to a free, democratic nation like the United States. We tried to focus our recommendations and conclusions on identifying and mitigating paradoxes and further illuminating ways to see hope rather than fear in our future. Fear is based on divisiveness and confusion rather than the hope of nurturing and healing. Fear is failure to prepare for the future and too often acts as a substitute for objective, positive outlooks. As a nation, we used to prefer the healing over the division and chaos that has confronted America in the last few years. We preferred hope and objectivity over fear and subjectivity.

To be sure, fear does overtake hope from time-to-time...it's part of an evolutionary survival system that pumps the right kinds of enzymes and hormones to the right places in our brains and bodies to give us an edge to escape a threat or think at an elevated level if we're able to harness those temporary advantages. Living in fear all the time or refusing to take advantage of normal thinking and activities produces stressors that ultimately put us at a disadvantage.[118] To choose to live in fear, when hope provides a much brighter outlook and allows for clearer and more objective thinking, is allowing primal emotions to negate the superior thinking ability with which humanity has been endowed. In other words, it makes little sense to prefer fear over hope, if we have a choice. The elections of November 2020 place before us one of the most important choices we as a nation have ever faced: do we choose hope, or do we prefer fear?

We used several of the essays to pose and frame "strategically important questions" about the topics discussed and how important good inquiry was to the process of discovering new directions and opportunities to do better by yourself, by your family, by your organizations, and no less importantly, how to do better by your nation. Good inquiry always guides us to the best answers. Good answers will in turn guide us to making better decisions about using our power to truly make America better.

We wanted to end this book with a call to action. We challenge our readers to become advocates for hope and positive change in America. We challenge you to use the lessons you've learned from reading about **Paradoxes of Power** to improve the balance and effectiveness of any power relationships you occupy, whether as a leader or a follower, and to use your personal power to support the needs of the many while also considering the needs of the few. We challenge you to look for power paradoxes all around you, and to help educate others about how we can avoid them. Finally, we challenge you to help yourself and others to avoid the influence of the "out of sight out of mind" mentality that has been the source of so many problems in this country. As John Lewis advised us, "When you see something that is not right, not just, not fair, you have a moral obligation to say something. To do something." If you find yourself inspired to meet even one of these challenges, we believe that we can say this book was a success.

Thank you for joining us in an exploration of **Paradoxes of Power** and considering how we might steer America on a path that brings us back to the ultimate vision of our Founders. They may not have gotten it perfect the first time around in 1787, but they wanted us to be able to get it right someday. They gave us the tools and the freedoms to do so, accompanied by an understanding of how important it was to build The **United** States of America. Now it's up to us to get the job done.

As a final note, our website, ParadoxesofPower.com, will remain operational for the foreseeable future to keep our interactions and your input accessible to as many as possible. Please visit and be a part of the future of our nation and its growth toward hope and equality.

Appendix A. The Essentials Of Power And Influence

by Walter E. Natemeyer[119]

Leadership and Power

This reading presents an overview of several key concepts related to leadership and power. It also provides a framework to help leaders assess the needs of their follower(s) and use the appropriate leadership styles and power bases in their influence attempts.

In 2001, my colleague Paul Hersey and I published an essay entitled "Situational Leadership and Power," in which we proposed that given the "integral relationship between leadership and power, leaders must not only assess their leader behavior in order to understand how they actually influence other people, but they must also examine their possession and use of power."[120] That is a fully packed proposition and one that defines the context of the entire discussion of power in this essay.

Our research on power is an expansion of the *Situational Leadership* model originally developed by Hersey and Kenneth Blanchard in 1969.[121] Situational Leadership calls for leaders to adapt their leadership styles (direction and support) according to the follower's "readiness level." It was one of the first models that demonstrated the importance of focusing on the follower's ability, willingness and confidence (Readiness Level) when selecting leadership styles. The key point of Situational Leadership is that there is no "one best leadership style" to effectively influence followers to do what the leader wants them to do. Hersey and I also contend that the follower's readiness level impacts which power bases will be most effective in the leader's influence attempts. We showed definitively that the application of power in an adaptive fashion was just as important as the situational approach to leadership styles.

Simply put, if leaders apply relevant and appropriate sources of power to a leader-follower relationship, they can avoid misfires in leadership, or what the editors and essayists of this book assert is a **Paradox of Power**. There's more to the power relationship than leadership style, readiness of followers and bases of power, but these are critically important components of the power relationship needed to avoid paradoxes. If leaders/wielders apply power correctly, they are more likely to use the appropriate leadership style as well.

Here's a bottom-line point about power relationships raised in this book: Leaders must have some sort of power to enable them to gain compliance and/or commitment from others. Of course, a corollary bottom line is that the follower must respond to that power for the compliance or commitment to be consummated. Matching followership readiness and power bases will greatly facilitate the style of leadership technique most likely to be effective in given situations. The upshot is that power is a potential force that binds together social relationships in an organizational environment. It may require the leader to be adaptive and situation oriented, but it offers leaders and organizations a better chance to avoid **Paradoxes of Power**.

Key Definitions

Common definitions of leadership and power in management literature are:

Leadership: The process of influencing the behavior of others in efforts toward goal accomplishment

Power: The potential for influence[122]

Let's look more closely at several concepts of power in the literature.

James MacGregor Burns wrote about power having two components: motive and resources. He described power as the motive to take some action combined with the resources to accomplish that action. Otherwise, power is only a potential just as in the physical world. The effective use of power leads to "transformational leadership," as Burns defined it. This approach to leadership and power "recognizes and exploits an existing need or demand of a potential follower...through a relationship of mutual stimulation and elevation."[123]

Burns clearly demonstrates the relevance of the power relationship that is mutually interdependent on both leader and follower. Leaders who understand how to use power are clearly more effective than those who do not. This was true before the advent of modern organizations, but in the face of relentless, adaptive threats to our organizations today, the effective use of power to coordinate and influence our people in the exercise of any type of operation is more critical than ever.

Definitions of Power as Practiced in Organizations

The concepts of leadership and power have generated lively interest, debate, and occasionally confusion throughout the evolution of management thought. As we pointed out earlier, power is closely related to leadership, for power is one of the means by which a leader influences the behavior of followers.[124] Given this integral relationship between leadership and power, leaders must not only assess their leader behavior in order to understand how they actually influence other people, but they must also examine their possession and use of power.[125]

I earlier defined leadership as an attempt to influence another individual or group and concluded that leadership is an influence process. Another way to think about this is that Power *is influence potential*—the resource that enables a leader to gain compliance or commitment from others. Despite its critical importance, power is a subject that is often avoided, for power can have an unpleasant side; many people may want to wish it away and pretend it is not there. But power is a real-world issue. Leaders who understand and know how to use power are more effective than those who do not or will not use power. To successfully influence the behavior of others, the leader should understand the impact of power on the various leadership styles. In today's world, many sources of power within organizations have been legislated, negotiated, or administered away. Leaders now have less of some types of power to draw from, so it is even more important to effectively use what is available. Because power bases drive leadership styles, using them appropriately can enhance your effectiveness as a leader.[126]

Position Power and Personal Power

One of the characteristics of leadership is that leaders exercise power. Amitai Etzioni discussed the difference between position power and personal power. His distinction resulted from his concept of power as the ability to induce or influence behavior. He claimed that power is derived from organizational position, personal influence, or both. Individuals who can induce other individuals to do a certain job because of their position in the organization are considered to have position power; individuals who derive their power from their followers are considered to have personal power. Some individuals have both position power and personal power.[127]

Where do managers get the position power that is available to them? Although Etzioni would argue that it comes from the organizational office of a manager, I think it comes from above the manager's office and, therefore, is not inherent in the office. Managers occupying positions in an organization may have more or less position power than their predecessors or someone else in a similar position in the same organization.

Position power is the extent to which those people to whom managers report are willing to delegate authority and responsibility down to them. So, position power tends to flow down in an organization; it is not just a matter of the office having power. This is not to say that leaders do not have any impact on how much position power they accrue. They certainly do. The confidence and trust they develop with the people above them will often determine the willingness of upper management to delegate down to them. And remember, whatever power is delegated downward can be taken back. We have all seen this occur when managers still have the same responsibilities, but their authority (to distribute rewards and sanctions) to get the job done has been taken away.

Personal power is the extent to which followers respect, like, and are committed to their leader and see their own goals as being satisfied by the goals of their leader. In other words, personal power is the extent to which people are willing to follow a leader. As a result, personal power in an organizational setting comes from below—from the followers—and so flows up in an organization. Thus, we must be careful when we say that some leaders are charismatic or have personal power that flows from them. Personal power is not inherent in the leader. If it were, managers with personal power could take over any department and have the same commitment and rapport they had in their last department. We know that they can't. Although managers certainly can influence the amount of personal power they have by the way they treat their people, it is a subjective and volatile kind of power. Followers can rapidly take it away. Make a few dramatic mistakes and see how many people are willing to follow. Personal power is a day-to-day phenomenon; it can be earned, and it can be taken away.

Etzioni suggested that the best situation for leaders is when they have both personal power and position power. Then the question becomes whether it is more important to have personal power or position power. In his 16th-century treatise *The Prince*, Niccolò Machiavelli presented an interesting viewpoint when he raised the question of whether it is better to have a relationship based on love (personal power) or fear (position power).[128] Machiavelli contended, as did Etzioni, that it is best to be both loved and feared. If, however, one cannot have both, he suggested that a relationship based on love alone tends to be volatile, short lived, and easily terminated when there is no fear of retaliation. On the other hand, a relationship based on fear tends to be longer lasting because the individual must be ready to incur the sanction (pay the price) before terminating the relationship.

This is a difficult concept for many people to accept. One of the most difficult roles for leaders—whether they be a supervisor, teacher, or parent—is disciplining someone about whom they care. Yet to be effective at enhancing others' growth and development, leaders sometimes must sacrifice short-term friendship for long-term respect. Machiavelli warned, however, that one should be careful that this fear (amount of position power) does not lead to hatred. Hatred often evokes overt behavior in terms of retaliation, undermining, and attempts to overthrow.

In summary, position power can be thought of as the authority, which is delegated down, to use rewards and sanctions. Personal power is the cohesiveness, commitment, and rapport between leaders and followers. It is also affected by the extent to which followers see their own goals as being the same, similar, or at least dependent on the accomplishment of the leader's goals.

Although personal and position power are distinct, ideally they are an interacting influence system. Often, followers are affected by their perceptions of both the leader's ability to provide rewards, punishments, and sanctions and the leader's ability to influence upward into the organization. The extent to which people above you in the organization are willing to delegate position power is often dependent on their perception of the followers' commitment to you. So, it is not sufficient to have either position or personal power alone—a leader needs to work at gaining both.

Other power base classification systems have been developed, but the framework devised by J. R. P. French and B. Raven appears to be the most widely accepted.[129], [130] They proposed that there are five bases of power:

coercive power

expert power

legitimate power

referent power and

reward power

Later, Raven and Kruglanski identified a sixth power base—**information power**.[131]

More recently, Hersey and Natemeyer proposed a seventh base of power—**connection power**.[132] We define each of these seven power bases in the next section.

Performance Readiness, Leadership Styles, and Power Bases

Hersey and Blanchard first developed Situational Leadership in the late 1960s. It is based on two key dimensions of leadership behavior: *providing direction* and *providing support*.[133] They developed a model that prescribed recommended forms of leadership behavior suited to the readiness levels of their followers. The interactive nature of leadership style and followership behaviors is key to their model.

<u>Directive Behavior</u> is the extent to which a leader defines roles for followers and explains what to do and when, where and how tasks are to be accomplished.

Supportive Behavior is the extent to which a leader builds and maintains positive relations with followers, characterized by effective 2-way communication, feedback, encouragement, praise and friendly interaction.

Let's review the relationship between performance readiness, leadership style, and the power base that drives that style. This is the heart of the discussion of the application of power.

Readiness Levels

R1 = Very Unable and/or Very Unwilling

R2 = Somewhat Unable but Willing

R3 = Able but Not Fully Confident or Not Fully Enthusiastic

R4 = Very Able, Willing and Confident

Leadership Styles

S1 = Above Average Direction and Below Average Supportive Behavior

S2 = Above Average Direction and Above Average Supportive Behavior

S3 = Below Average Direction and Above Average Supportive Behavior

S4 = Below Average Direction and Below Average Supportive Behavior

Key Power Bases

Coercive Power—The Perceived Ability to Provide Negative Consequences for Not Performing

Followers at performance readiness level R1 need guidance and direction. Too much supportive behavior with people at this level who are not currently performing may be perceived as permissive or as rewarding the lack of performance. Without some coercive power to drive the leadership "telling style" (S1), attempts to influence will most likely be ineffective. Followers who don't perform need to know that if they do not respond appropriately, there may be some costs, problems, sanctions or other negative consequences. These may take the form of a reprimand, cut in pay, transfer, demotion, or even termination.

As we'll discuss below on potential failings of power, it's worth noting here that managers often erode their coercive power by not following through. They may, for instance, have the ability to impose sanctions, but for one reason or another be unwilling to do so. This reluctance to use sanctions can result in a loss of power. Another way to erode coercive power is by not differentiating the use of sanctions based on performance. If people feel that they will be punished regardless of performance, coercive power has little impact on a leader's ability to influence them.

It is even possible to "talk" coercive power away. Let's say that a manager begins a performance appraisal interview with a low performer by saying, "Now, look, both of us know that you've been here over 20 years and I can't fire you." In those few words, the manager has stripped away any coercive power the follower might have perceived.

Connection Power—The Perceived Association of the Leader with Influential Persons or Organizations

Connection power is an important driver for "telling" (S1) and "selling" (S2) leadership styles. Usually, followers at R1 and R2 want to avoid the sanctions or gain the favor they associate with powerful connections. The important issue is not whether there is a real connection, but whether there is a perception of a real connection.

For example, a first-level supervisor may be regarded as having limited power. But if that supervisor is highly respected throughout the organization or is married to a relative of the company president, the perceived connection may provide added influence with others in the organization.

Reward Power—The Perceived Ability to Provide Things That People Would Like to Have

Reward power is enhanced if followers perceive managers as having the ability to give appropriate rewards. Followers who are unable to currently perform a certain task but are willing to make an effort (R2) are most likely to try on new behaviors if they feel increases in performance will be rewarded. Rewards may include raises, bonuses, promotions, or transfers to more desirable positions. They may also include intangibles such as a pat on the back or feedback on accomplishment. In the final analysis, managers get what they reward. Therefore, it matters not only that the reward be offered in a timely manner, but also that the reward be perceived as such by the receiver. More pointedly, what constitutes a reward is indeed in the eye of the beholder.

A significant amount of reward power has been legislated, negotiated, and administered away over the past few decades. This has resulted from companies endeavoring to avoid costly litigation when they are forced to downsize, restructure, and cut costs in response to the increasingly competitive global environment. Consequently, we often must remind managers that reward power is tied to not only monetary rewards. This may require some creative thinking, but discovering what intangibles truly motivate followers can have an enormous impact on a leader's reward power. Managers, however, often erode what little reward power they have by making promises they don't keep. Consider, for example, the following:

Salesperson: I did it! I made the 15 percent over quota with room to spare. When am I going to get that 10 percent bonus?

Sales Manager: I'm sorry, but economic conditions are such that we'll have to postpone it for a while. But don't worry, if you keep up the good work, I promise I'll make it up to you.

Other managers erode their reward power by "hoping for A

but rewarding B."[134] An example might be an organization that gives all salespeople a 10 percent cost-of-living adjustment and yet the difference between reward for average sales and outstanding sales is only 1 or 2 percent. In this case, "hanging around" for another year is significantly rewarded. This practice often results in high performers losing their motivation and commitment or looking outside the company for opportunities. A problem with power derived from rewards is that rewards will often run their course. The manager will be left with an employee who is no longer motivated by rewards and an organization that can no longer provide relevant rewards.

Legitimate Power – The Perception that the Leader has the Right to Make Decisions because of Title, Role or Position in the Organization

Legitimate power can be a useful driver for both the selling and participating leadership styles but ineffective for followers who are both unable and unwilling or insecure (R1). They may not care whether someone's title is supervisor or manager. Similarly, followers high in performance readiness (R4) are far less impressed with title or position than they are with the leader's expertise or information. However, followers in the moderate ranges of performance readiness (R2 or R3) can often be influenced if they feel it is appropriate for a person in that position with that title to make that decision. For example, a salesperson might comment to a peer about the department's recent reorganization: "Pat should be making those kinds of decisions...that's what the sales manager gets paid to do."

Referent Power—The Perceived Attractiveness of Interacting with the Leader

In attempting to influence people who are able but insecure or unwilling (R3), high-relationship behavior is necessary. If people have a confidence problem, the manager needs to provide encouragement. If they have a motivation problem, the manager needs to discuss and problem-solve. In either case, if the manager has not taken time to build rapport, attempts to participate may be perceived as adversarial rather than helpful. Confidence, trust, and rapport are important ingredients necessary for influencing people. If a follower feels that the manager will provide encouragement and help when it is needed, referent power can make an important difference in the success of the influence attempt. Referent power is based on the manager's personal traits, such as integrity and honesty. A manager high in referent power is generally liked and admired by others because of personality. It is this liking of, admiration for, and identification with the manager that influences others.

Information Power—The Perceived Access to, or Possession of, Useful Information

The styles that tend to effectively influence followers at above-average performance readiness levels (R3 and R4) are participating (S3) and delegating (S4). Information power is most helpful in driving these leadership styles. The importance of this power source has grown significantly with the rapid development of and access to information technology. In fact, it has continued to grow in importance as more data becomes available and accessible. Those who know how to access the information needed in a timely manner tend to be the ones that others seek out, and sharing that information provides an opportunity for those knowledge holders to influence the behaviors of others.

Information power is based on *perceived access to data*. This is different from expert power, which is the understanding of or ability to use data. For example, one study found that some employees in a major corporate office had a significant amount of information power but little expert power in some technical areas. These influencers were able to help gain access to information, but had little expertise themselves.

Expert Power—The Perception That the Leader Has Relevant Education, Experience, and Expertise

Followers who are competent and confident require little direction or supportive behavior. They are able and willing to perform on their own. The driver for influencing these followers is expert power. With followers who are able and confidently willing (R4), leaders are more effective if they possess the expertise, skill, and knowledge that followers respect and regard as important. An apt example is Al Smith, former governor of New York State. When he was a freshman legislator, he spent his nights studying the New York State budget instead of attending the many social events. As Tom Peters, well-known author and commentator on the management scene, described it, "His matchless command of the fine print [of the budget] launched an extraordinary career."[135]

In summarizing a review of the most important research relating supervisory power bases to follower satisfaction and performance, I reached the following general conclusion: Although expert and legitimate power bases appear to be the most important reasons for compliance, and expert and referent power bases tend to be strongly and consistently related to follower performance and satisfaction measures, the results are not clear enough to generalize about a best power base.[136] In fact, the results suggest that the appropriate power base is largely affected by situational variables. In other words, leaders may need various power bases, depending on the situation.

Figure A-1, below, relates the types of power bases I described above to the Readiness Levels of Followers. The important thing about this depiction is that it recommends or prescribes certain power bases that correspond with the follower's Readiness Level, noted as "R4" through "R1," where a follower is most prepared and motivated to perform a mission or task shown as an R4. R1 levels depict a follower who may be neither prepared nor motivated, often through no fault of their own. These followers are ill-equipped to contribute much to the power relationship, whereas an R4 may be an outstanding contributor to the relationship.

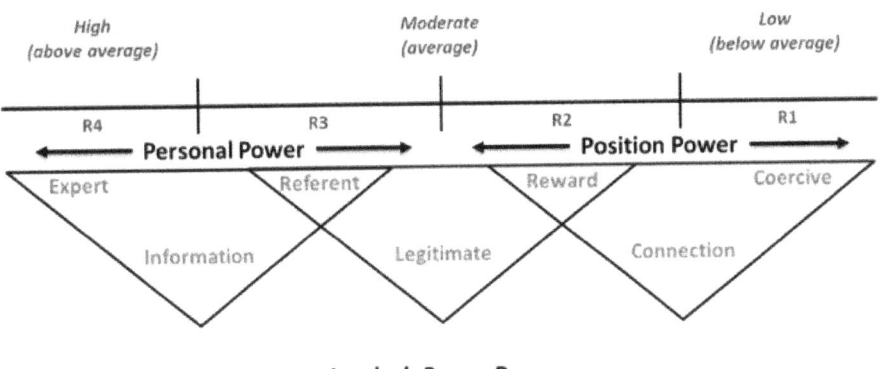

Figure A-1 - Power Bases and Readiness of Followers, by Walter E. Natemeyer and Carl W. Hunt

Power Bases and Performance Readiness Level

Hersey, Blanchard and I proposed that there is a direct relationship between the level of performance readiness of individuals and groups and the kind of power bases that have a high probability of gaining compliance from those people.[137] Situational Leadership views performance readiness as the ability and willingness of individuals or groups to take responsibility for directing their own behavior in a particular situation. Thus, it must be reemphasized that performance readiness is a task-specific concept and depends on what the leader is attempting to accomplish.

As people move from lower to higher levels of performance readiness, their competence and confidence to do things increase. The seven power bases appear to have significant impact on the behavior of people at various levels of performance readiness, as seen in Figure A-1.

In Chapter 1, Carl and Joshua Hunt referred to the other elements of the power relationship apart from only the wielder and the yielder. This chapter, "Power and Paradox," expands on this topic but it's worth reviewing a bit to point out that leadership, followership, power and influence all combine and interact to build and strengthen the power relationship; this points even further to the social nature of power. Culture, organizational climate, readiness of both leaders and followers, technology and even policy and polity influence how the wielder and yielder interact in this relationship. Certainly, the notion of trust between leader and follower is essential, as well.

This goes back to Burns' thinking about relationships that are bound by motives and constraints, his two "essentials of power." Building the connections of power, based on the motives of the leader and the constraints of the organizational environment achieve what we call today win-win relationships. "To define power not as a property or entity or possession but as a relationship in which two or more persons tap motivational bases in one another and bring varying resources to bear in the process is to perceive power as drawing a vast range of human behavior into its orbit," wrote Burns.[138]

The idea of achieving win-win relationships between all the players in the power relationship serves to magnify the positive outcomes that emerge between wielders of power and yielders to power, leaders and followers, principals and adherents, stars and fans. Burns also suggested this in his descriptions of what he called *transformational leadership*.[139] Humility and appreciation for each other to help all the participants in the relationship can produce much greater good than simply being in the game only for oneself. That's the very essence of a transformative power relationship.

Carl and Joshua also discussed this "greater good" in terms of emergent behaviors that demonstrate behavior that is greater than the sum of its parts in Chapter 1. We can all exercise power in these relationships if we take ownership and serve in humility and nurturing strength. In fact, Burns even wrote that "leadership is a special form of power." We treat the two terms separately in this book, but it's challenging to separate the extended case of *good* leadership and *good* power relationships as they are fully interdependent on each other and consistently reflect nurture and humility.[140]

When Power Fails – The Roots of Paradox[141]

There are three main categories of power failure in the social partnership between leader and follower: erosion of power; mismatched use of power; and abuse of power. All three can result in a paradox that disrupts the organization, the follower and/or the leader. A misfire in any of the failings of power can lead to damage or even the downfall of the organization, and in the case of an abuse of power even an entire nation. In this section, we'll briefly examine erosion and mismatch of power.

Eroding Sources of Power[142]

We discussed a few instances of erosion of power in the examples of each power base above. Here are some more to consider. Since leaders have only a limited amount of power available to them, one would hope that they would hold on to whatever power bases they have. Yet some leaders who start off with significant power gradually lose their power. The key to avoiding such erosion is to cultivate and utilize your power bases.

For example, a leader could have a significant amount of coercive power but gradually lose it by threatening followers with punishment and not following through. In this context, people will start to think that the leader really does not have any coercive power. Similarly, leaders can lose their reward power if everyone gets the same reward whether they perform or not, or just because they have seniority in industry. Some parents establish age requirements when kids can get to do things. "When you're 13, you'll be able to stay out past 10 o'clock. When you're 16, you'll be able to stay home alone." The problem with using age as a factor in determining when people can do things is that all they must do is get older. When age is used as the determining factor, reward power as a parent or a leader is lost because what is happening is that people are getting rewards for being older, not for being more ready to take responsibility.

Connection power can be eroded when people begin to see that the sponsor or connection does not make any disciplinary interventions or provide any favors or sanctions. In other words, to be maintained, connection power needs occasional interventions from the sponsor. Similarly, managers can lose their legitimate power failing to make decisions that people think they ought to make, given their position. Erosion of this power base can also occur if a manager continually makes decisions that are not fruitful. After a while, their staff members will no longer look to them to make decisions even if they have the title of senior research scientist or department manager.

This erosion process also works against referent power. When you give praise or recognition to those who are performing and the same praise or recognition to those who are not performing, you begin to erode your referent power. If people do not have to earn praise and recognition, then you no longer have referent power.

Leaders must also be careful about eroding their information and expert power, particularly if they give away expertise and information to people whose goals are not organizational goals. If you give away too much information and knowledge, eventually those people will not need you. The only way you can get around this problem is to continually develop new information and new expertise, so followers return to their sources.

If leaders let their power bases erode, they will also reduce the effectiveness of their leadership attempts. For example, an effective telling (S1) leadership style depends on having some coercive power. If leaders are perceived as unable to deliver punishments and sanctions, their use of that style is limited.

The same can be said about a selling (S2) style. Without some control over rewards, leaders may not be able to reinforce or compensate for increased performance as followers grow and develop their skills. This applies more to R1s and R2s, as by the time followers are R3 and R4, the leader should be actively helping to grow these more experienced followers into leadership positions.

A participating (S3) style won't work if people don't like and respect a manager. Additionally, if a manager has let reward power erode by not being particularly responsive to people, then a participative, high-relationship style might not be seen as a reward, but as a punishment. Suppose a manager has ignored a staff member for a long time then, suddenly, when that person's family life begins to deteriorate, the manager tries to comfort and console the staffer. Since the manager has eroded available referent power, time with the boss is not seen as a positive experience.

A manager who is supervising highly competent and motivated people needs to have some expert power to make any kind of significant intervention. If the manager has eroded information and expert power, the possibility of influencing these people in any significant way will be limited.
The two charts below capture the main characteristics of *Building* and *Losing* (Eroding) power in leadership functions. These characteristics apply in all leadership positions whether applying personal or position powers:

Power Base	**Characteristics of Building Power**
Coercive	Hold people accountable
	Administer sanctions
	Provide feedback
	Say "Not good enough!"
	Say "If you don't do it…"

	Reprimand or Fire Negative performance appraisal
Connection	Network with boss and others within organization Seek opportunities to do cross-functional work Name dropping Network outside the organization
Reward	Provide Praise Say "Thanks" Utilize rewards appropriately MBWA* to monitor and recognize performance
Legitimate	Verbalize your authority Utilize your authority Explain your actions and decisions
Referent	Admit mistakes Talk to people (including one-on-one) MBWA* Be friendly and approachable / Adopt Positive body language Be Patient / Ask questions / Solicit input Always demonstrate Integrity Be professional Share knowledge / experience
Information	Listen / Share information from your leaders / Ask for input and feedback Maximize your access to information through personal and virtual networking Stay current in your field / organization Utilize your own connections to stay "in the know"

Expert	Continuously develop / share your technical and managerial expertise
	Share yours and others' experiences
	Become and stay a Subject Matter Expert
	Earn certifications / degrees, etc.
	Educate / Train others
	Build track record for making good decisions

* Management by Walking Around

Power Base	Characteristics of Losing Power
Coercive	Fail to hold people accountable
	Threaten and not follow through with consequences
Connection	Fail to build new connections as people move, retire, etc.
	Break trust with your connections
Reward	Play favorites
	Overuse rewards
	Underuse rewards
Legitimate	"My Way or the Highway" mentality
	Underutilize your authority
	Overstep your limits of authority
Referent	Demonstrate favoritism
	Fail to be genuine / sincere
	Share too much information
Information	Hoard information
	Use information to promote a hidden agenda
	Provide inaccurate information
	Lie / misspeak

	Share too much information
Expert	Stop learning
	Consistently Make wrong decisions
	Fail to listen to others

Mismatched Use of Power

Mismatched use of power, or just misuse of power in the benign sense, is just what it sounds like. In the case of a business environment, as an illustration, leaders/wielders of power might use coercion when they should be using referent or information power. Referring to Figure A-1, a mismatch of this instance could occur when a follower is R3 or R4 and the boss attempts to threaten or intimidate through coercion. This is plainly a failure of the power relationship and it's almost exclusively the boss's shortcoming. The leader should be better aware of the employee's capability or motivation and apply the appropriate power base accordingly. The leader can't expect their followers to stay motivated for long under those circumstances.

Another example of misuse of power might be when the boss treats a group of R1s as though they were R3s or R4s. In this case, the leader might give the R1s free reign, with no guidance whatsoever, to accomplish a complex or mission-critical task. It's not hard to imagine that unless the best of luck prevails, the followers and the task will fail. No one in the organization succeeds in that scenario and instead of a win-win situation, the boss has created a lose-lose condition. Guess who pays for that!

Leadership and maintenance of effective power relationships is hard work. That's why good leaders are compensated and have opportunities to lead at higher and higher levels. Plus, the best leaders provide paths and models for followers to become good leaders too. This winning situation occurs only when power works in an effective, fully interconnected relationship. Effective power relationships are the heart of all successfully functioning organizations regardless of size or purpose.

Abuse of Power

The abuse of power, whether intentional or accidental (often accompanied by the other two, Mismatch and Erosion), is among the biggest threats facing the United States in the last few decades. It's also a primary source for the paradoxes we discussed in the essays of this book, beginning with Chapter 1. Chapter 1 and the ensuing essays offer extensive discussions on abuse of power.

Every time we form some sort of connection, either temporary or permanent, the members of the relationship practice wielding and yielding power. When you are the wielder, think about how the other partners in the relationship perceive you and assist you to accomplish the goals of that relationship. Be humble in exercising power...to semi-quote the "Golden Rule," treat others as you would like them to treat you. Leaders (and followers): *Use Your Power for Good!*

Appendix B. Complexity And Emergence

by Carl W. Hunt

This appendix addresses two main and recurring themes throughout this book: *complexity* and *emergence*, particularly as these concepts relate to the use and misuse of power. While these two terms have a specific scientific basis, especially in biology and life sciences, we will generalize a bit here and there in order to make their contributions to comprehending power more accessible to those who would rather not revisit their biology textbooks.

Complexity

Let's get oriented to these ideas first. We'll begin with a simple graphic, Figure B-1, below. This graphic helps explain what we might call "domains of orientation" to any type of event, whether related to leadership or any other behavior. These domains of orientation include simple, complicated, complex and chaotic.[143]

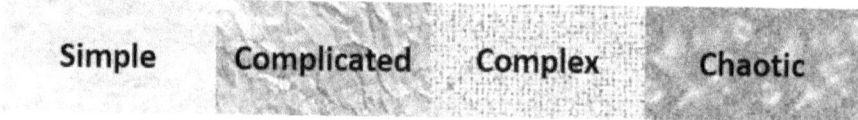

Figure B-1: Four Domains of Orientation to Power, by Carl W. Hunt

Briefly, a simple domain is essentially "what you see is what you get," as the old saying goes. If this domain were a landscape, it would be flat and easy to understand what it contains; it's mostly predictable in terms of what to expect to occur next in the environment. A complicated domain has more hills...more peaks and valleys to obscure events or information, but it's not all that challenging to understand the overall viewpoint and the relationship of cause and effect of what's going on, even if we must look harder. It can help to "think outside of the box" to better orient to this environment, but we can still succeed by taking the time to explore the nooks and crannies of this world.

The complex domain, the main subject of this discussion, is just chock full of interactions of the components that make up this environment. Where it was straightforward to observe the cause and effect relationships in a complicated setting, that's not true in a complex world. Management theorist Nick Obolensky writes that a complex environment is one in which "cause and effect are combined. The multiple 'agents' involved (for example, people, organizations, technological component parts of the system and so on) are interconnected with feedback loops that affect each other in a complex network that is hard to predict." [144] Another way to think about such a setting is to visualize a pattern-rich domain where the observer has to trace each end of each link, including interconnections, to see where it goes and how it fits within the overall picture. It doesn't take long to lose orientation or focus when trying to figure out a complex environment, but oftentimes the learning is in the doing. While we may never understand a complex system, we might learn enough to see the patterns and more reliably predict outcomes. That's what we seek in trying to appreciate complexity in **Paradoxes of Power**.

Resolving complexity requires an understanding of emergence, a term on which we expand below. For now, in relationship to understanding power and paradox as an emergence, keep in mind the simple definition of emergence as a behavior or object that exceeds the sum of its parts. More on that shortly.

Military schools taught this old soldier that recognizing chaos means there could be opportunities available that others might not see if they're not comfortable in such an environment. That's the best we can hope for in the final domain of the graphic above. It's even more difficult to visualize and orient to the expressions of leadership and power in the chaotic environment. This is "rare and is where there is no discernible cause and effect at all." Obolensky, writes that there are "no manageable patterns – only turbulence."[145] Here the leader's main job is not to find patterns, but "stop the bleeding" and allow the team or organization to get back into the game as soon as possible and move towards a domain in which the organization can get things under some semblance of control. In scientific terms, chaos is a well-studied state and it is currently unclear that normal operations in the chaotic environment are even possible for long. Many speculate that the United States has been in chaos for the last 3½ years, although I believe we've drifted in and out of it from the beginning.

Organizations can thrive in simple and complicated environments, and if they can master complex environments they may even succeed beyond all expectations. Chaos, however, may not only be debilitating but destructive, and it should be avoided or at least mitigated if at all possible.

We initially challenged ourselves to define what a paradox is as it relates to power, and to come up with examples to discuss throughout the book. To expand on the definitions described in Walt Natemeyer's explanation of power in organizations in Appendix A, a **Paradox of Power** is just what it is in any other setting. A paradox is a "self-contradictory statement" that is typically unacceptable with regard to logic, but yet has some appeal to the reasoning process.[146] This is because on a paradox's surface, conclusions appear to fit a logical framework and they initially may sound like they make sense, even if we don't understand the statement or event. But given it is a self-contradiction, we know that the statement or event is in fact not logical. Sounds complex, doesn't it? This is where understanding paradoxes in light of complexity and emergence is helpful.

Emergence

The notion of achieving something "greater than the sum of its parts" should be at the heart of any significant organizational mission statement. After all, leaders build organizations to harness the talents, gifts and experiences of all their team members if they truly want to succeed. Understanding power and achievement as emergent phenomena, and part of a richly complex network of relationships, helps leaders of organizations achieve greater things. Contemplating the emergence of both power and paradoxes within such an environment is a key motivator for applying a little bit of behavioral and biological science to our study and this book.

Being comfortable with the concept of emergence in an organization or power situation entails an appreciation that sometimes things happen, or people behave in what appear to be totally unpredictable ways. This is sometimes referred to as an object being more than the sum of its parts, and where even a full comprehension of each of those parts does not lead to a full awareness of their interactions and ultimate behaviors. For example, individual follower behaviors in a group do not always inform leaders as to what will happen when these individuals interact and resulting team behaviors occur. We saw this in recounting the story of the Abilene Paradox in Chapter 1.

In my own experience, emergence can also describe a behavior that is surprisingly paradoxical. "Abilene" shows us a type of emergence where the behavior that results from group deliberation reflected nothing that any of the individual parts desired. You could almost say the sum was far *less* than that of any individual part, because not a single person got what they actually wanted. This demonstrates an emergence of negative behavior, and one that could be easily avoided if the group members possessed any kind of understanding of what was happening and attempted to communicate effectively with each other.

Although Harvey doesn't describe it that way, his story provides us with a formal, repeatable example of a truly counterintuitive behavioral emergence. In fact, each of the examples of paradox we cited throughout the book could be considered the same way. Emergence and organizational paradox have a lot in common. No one in the Abilene example wanted to go to the diner, but everyone willingly piled into the hot dusty car and headed off to a totally dissatisfying meal anyway. This was an emergent behavior, plain and "simple!"

We often think we can definitively prepare for how relationships within organizations begin and work out through their life span. We formulate plans, resource them, and train with our people to execute them as effectively as possible. Unfortunately, in doing so we fail to recognize a true paradox, stated succinctly by Dwight D. Eisenhower, US President and Five-Star Army general: "Plans are worthless, but planning is everything," Ike wisely observed.[147] Planning, as a practice to visualize requirements, helps us understand what we need to succeed in human relationships. No plan survives first contact with the enemy, as we used to say in the Army (and probably many other types of organizations).

Plans rarely come off the way we envision them, and this specifically applies to power relationships between leaders and followers, the people who execute the plans. What highly successful leaders discover is that leadership behavior is not in fact about themselves. Rather it is informed by the readiness of their followers, the organizational mission, the law, the rules and regulations imposed by the group's authority, and a host of other factors that leaders should weigh before deciding how to exercise power. The scope of the organization's reach is important as well because it imposes constraints that only experience and a willingness to adapt could possibly overcome. It is all extraordinarily complex; good leadership is hard work, and effective balance of power in the wielder-yielder relationship is equally challenging. Smart leaders rarely rely on the specific details of the plan. What we truly need for success ultimately unfolds as we try to execute the plan…it emerges. If we're prepared, it's because of the planning process, but surprises can still crop up from any direction.

Studying complex systems, organizational paradox, and emergence together is important because human power interactions comprise all three. Leaders and followers both need to understand the basics of these concepts so that we can recognize, plan for, and hopefully avoid malfunctioning power connections, or deal with them if they do arise. Leaders may think their organizations aren't sophisticated enough to benefit from understanding these concepts, but they may be selling their followers short if they don't at least try to create more effective power relationships. If they don't, leaders may repeatedly run into scenarios that are entirely too common, where avoidable paradoxes have become the norm in the typical organizational environment. That's an emergence none of us want.

About The Authors

Carl W. Hunt is a retired US Army colonel and former consultant to various agencies of the US Government. He is a graduate of the National Defense University's National War College. In his early working years, he was a police officer in Houston, Texas and an enlisted military policeman and criminal investigator in the US Army. He holds a Master of Science in National Security Strategy from the National Defense University and a Ph.D. in Information Technology from George Mason University.

Dr. Hunt has published numerous papers, articles and blog posts about the socio-technological convergence our nation and the world are experiencing in cyberspace. Much of his writing is devoted to leadership and education in both physical and virtual environments. Dr. Hunt led interagency research efforts in developing advanced collaboration models and technologies that helped shape the evolution of cyberspace operations and security in both military and civilian communities.

Walter E. Natemeyer, Founder and CEO of North American Training and Development, Inc., is an internationally recognized management author, consultant and educator. He received his BBA and MBA degrees from Ohio University and his Ph.D. in Organizational Behavior from the University of Houston. He has taught Leadership courses in the MBA Programs at the University of Chicago Booth School of Business and Nova Southeastern University and is the recipient of numerous teaching excellence awards.

Dr. Natemeyer is a leading authority on "Situational Leadership and Power," employee motivation, strategic planning and team building. He has authored numerous books, articles, and training instruments on these and other management topics, and has designed and conducted management development programs for more than 100 major organizations in the USA and abroad including Alcoa, American Petroleum Institute, American Red Cross, Apache Corporation, Aramco, Baylor College of Medicine, BP, Calpine, Chase Bank, and NASA, to name just a few.

Lawrence A. Kuznar (Emeritus Professor of Anthropology, Purdue University-Fort Wayne) received his PhD in anthropology and an MS in mathematical methods in the social sciences from Northwestern University and was a faculty member at PFW from 1990 to 2020. His areas of expertise include the domestication of plants and animals, tribal conflict, computational modeling, discourse analysis, counterterrorism and national security studies.

Over his career he has conducted field research in the South-American Andes and on the Navajo Reservation in the southwestern United States. His early research concerned the domestication of plants and animals and the rise of social complexity. He went on to study tribal conflict and to develop mathematical and computational models of conflict and social unrest. For the past 15 years, Dr. Kuznar has conducted research in support of counterterrorism, strategic planning and national security challenges for the U.S. government. His most recent research focuses on analyzing how the language of terrorists and world leaders reveals motivations, values and anticipates their future actions.

Dennis W. Greene serves as CEO of the Denver Technological Center/Greenwood Village Chamber of Commerce, noted as one of the top 30 economic zones in the United States, located in the Denver, Colorado metropolitan area. Greene's selection follows a 32-year Air Force career, spanning from May 1979 through June 2011, retiring in the rank of Colonel, followed by a career in the Federal Civil Service, totaling over 40 years continuous service to his country.

Dennis received his associate's degree in Administrative Management from the Community College of the Air Force, and his bachelor's degree in Business Management from Charleston Southern University, in Charleston South Carolina, earning honors as a Distinguished ROTC graduate. He received his master's degree with honors in Human Resources Management from Troy State University, in Montgomery Alabama, and a second Master's in Strategic Studies from Air University, while a student at Air War College, Maxwell Air Force Base, Alabama.

Marc Hill is a passionate member and supporter of the Black Lives Matter movement with an emphasis on the fact that **all black lives matter**. He is an outspoken protestor of police brutality, inequality, and political unbalance in the United States and abroad. An empathetic fighter in the ongoing battle against systemic racism, Marc maintains that he "is not here to belittle, but to educate and inform about what's truly wrong with this country."

Marc holds a Bachelor's degree in Biology, and has split his time over the last decade between roles in IT, sales, and small business entrepreneurship. He is an accomplished personal fitness trainer and recently started his own fitness + activism clothing line, Wolfheart LLC, from which a portion of the proceeds benefit the Colorado Wolf and Wildlife sanctuary.

C.E. Hunt, a 5th-generation Texan, has been involved in the conservation of our nation's natural and cultural resources since 1989 both in the US and abroad. He has lived and traveled across North America and Europe. Along with serving as a Presidential Management Intern upon the completion of his graduate degree, his non-writing career has included assignments with numerous conservation agencies, including the Texas A&M Sea Grant, National Park Service, Bureau of Land Management, National Oceanic and Atmospheric Service and Bureau of Reclamation. His work has been published by Texas A&M University Press, University of Texas Press and the Houston Chronicle.

One of his greatest passions is to help people see the value of nature and wild places. He's written extensively on the need to conserve nature in his native Texas, including the Big Thicket, Neches River, Trans-Pecos (Big Bend) Region and the Texas Hill Country. He published his first work of fiction in 2020, titled *A Moveable Marfa* with a sequel, *The Sommières Sun*, scheduled to be published in the spring of 2021. He holds a Masters Degree in Public Administration from Texas A&M University.

Veronica A. Mata is the manager and operations director for a locally owned Colorado small business that has seen growth and success since it opened its doors in 2014. She has worked in and supported various small businesses for the last decade and has an undeniable passion for helping grow those businesses and the communities they are a part of. In 2020, she founded her own company: Local Buzz - Small Business Solutions, whose mission is to make the dream of owning and operating a successful small company in the modern world of e-commerce and social media one that is attainable for everyone.

Veronica is a strong supporter of equality and particularly the advancement of women of all races around the world. She sincerely hopes that by bringing attention to the power paradoxes that affect women and minorities in the United States, we, as members of the global population, can learn to grow and move forward together, supporting one another rather than holding each other back.

Joshua M. Hunt. Like so many other millennials, Josh's work experience is a bit of a mixed bag. He has worked in the small business sector since the age of 15, and in the decade and a half that followed, he has held roles in management, operations, and marketing. He has worked as a bicycle repair technician, a certified personal trainer, a director of operations, and a bartender, and did a couple of years in corporate sales, just to see what "the big business side of things" looked like. He didn't care for it, and now works as a writer/editor and small business consultant in addition to studying web coding and application development at Colorado State University.

Josh initially graduated with a Bachelor's degree in Biology, and spends his free time writing and researching across a wide variety of current events. He is an advocate for fairness and equality, and a steadfast supporter of social distancing and wearing a mask in public for the safety of others. Josh believes that there is a lot of paradoxical behavior in this country right now, but he is hopeful that with the right awareness, activism, and education, we can all work together to fix it.

Acknowledgements

In the previous section we identified the main essayists and a little about their diverse backgrounds. These writers were the primary contributors to Paradoxes of Power. We are sincerely grateful for their contributions and the diversity and depth of the knowledge and experience they bring to this collection of essays. Thank you, Walt, Veronica, Dennis, Marc, Larry and CE.

Carl has known Walt since 1982 when Walt was his grad school advisor at the University of Houston, Clear Lake, and they are still close friends. Larry and Carl have been friends since Carl retired from the Army in 2006, and he has kept Carl's thinking focused and at least pseudo-academic ever since. This book kicked off formally with Dennis and Carl at breakfast in Centennial, CO, on July 2, 2020. Veronica is Josh's amazing wife and therefore, she is Carl's incredible daughter-in-law; Veronica and Josh own Local Buzz Business Solutions, LLC, of Centennial, CO, the producer of this book. CE—Carl's brother—has been one of Carl's best friends and writing partners for years. Marc is a remarkable young man, and one of Josh's best friends. Thanks to all of you: your work was absolutely terrific and deeply insightful in helping our readers understand **Paradoxes of Power**.

There were others, however, and in every way, no less important contributors. First, we must recognize the influence of Dr. Stuart Kauffman, MD, who has inspired and mentored both of us. Stu has been a great friend and colleague through many years. Stu was the co-advisor on Carl's doctoral dissertation and responsible for teaching Carl "to think like a scientist." Thanks, Stu!

Dr. David A. Schum and Dr. David Davis have been great friends and advisors over the last 20 years. Sadly, both recently passed, but their influence and inspiration live on. Dave Schum was Carl's academic advisor and dissertation co-director at George Mason University; Dave Davis was a co-worker dating back to 2004. Both gentlemen, and they were true gentlemen, were natural philosophers in the best sense, and taught Carl and ultimately Josh much about the art and science of inquiry. We're glad they live on in both of our memories.

We also want to recognize the contributions of Vanessa Veazie, our primary copy editor for **Paradoxes of Power**. Vanessa filled this important role just in time to ensure we could publish the book before the elections of 2020. This was always our goal and Vanessa made it possible to produce this collection of essays that, if there is any polish to it, the fit and finish is due to her diligence along with the great creativity of the essayists.

We also want to thank Carl's friends Wayne Porter and Todd Veazie, both retired US Navy Captains, and both still contributing greatly to our nation's security and prosperity. Wayne is one of the principal authors of "A National Strategic Narrative" as highlighted in Chapter 10. Todd and Carl have been big fans of Wayne's work over the years. Todd, also a fellow National War College graduate from Carl's class of 2003, has been another of Carl's best friends over the years; they've discussed many of the important issues we present in the book, and while not always agreeing, the discussions were always robust and motivating! Also, Carl must thank Colonel (USAF, ret.) Joseph J. Eash, III, for his support over the last 20 years as a friend and mentor— Joe wrote one the most moving blog posts on the Paradoxes of Power website, reflecting his love for family and country, and inspiring a great many readers.

Most importantly, we must sincerely thank Barbara Hunt, Carl's wife, and Josh's mom (and Veronica's mother-in-law). Barbara read every word (multiple times) and provided so many terrific edits and additional suggestions to improve **Paradoxes of Power** and the blog posts we've written that highlight the ideas we present in the book. We are immensely grateful to her! And, we love her!

Speaking of blog posts, we've kept paradoxesofpower.com online throughout the creation of the book and intend to keep the ideas we've discussed alive for some time after its publication. Please keep an eye on the website for updates and a refresh of the book as we proceed through the election of 2020 and beyond.

- Carl and Joshua
September 15, 2020

End Notes

[1] Hersey, P., and Natemeyer, W., "Situational Leadership and Power," *Classics of Organizational Behavior*, Waveland Press, Long Grove IL, 2011.

[2] For the most recent textbook-based presentation on "Situational Leadership," see Hersey, P., Blanchard., K, et. al., *Management of Organizational Behavior*, 10th Edition, Pearson Education, Inc., Saddle River, NJ, 2013.

[3] Natemeyer, W. "An Empirical Investigation" collected for use by North American Training and Development, Inc.

[4] Hunt, C., Kuznar, L., Kauffman, S., "Why politics is so polarized, even though Americans agree on most key issues," Oxford University Press Blog, June 13, 2020.

[5] Groupthink is a phenomenon where the members of the group are typically unaware of the gravity of the decision they are making, and a strong leader dominates the decision-making process. There is an illuminating contrast in Groupthink & Abilene Paradox. The differences may seem subtle, but the implications are different.

[6] Quoted from "An Abilene Defense: Commentary One," by Rosabeth Moss Kanter (page 37), extracted from a collection of updated perspectives and defenses against the paradox in "The Abilene Paradox: The Management of Agreement," written by Jerry B. Harvey, 1974, and collected in an undated document, posted at: http://homepages.se.edu/cvonbergen/files/2013/01/The-Abilene-Paradox_The-Management-of-Agreement.htm_.pdf. The Harvey essay also appeared in his book, *The Abilene Paradox and other Meditations on Management*, by Jerry B. Harvey, Jossey-Bass, San Francisco, CA, 1988.

[7] *Op. cit.*, See also a video of a chatty presentation of "The Abilene Paradox" Dr. Harvey made to the Defense Systems Management Course at Ft. Belvoir, VA, 1981.

[8] This is further explained in detail in Appendix A, through the application of "Situational Power" as Walt Natemeyer demonstrates.

[9] *Ibid.*, Harvey, *The Abilene Paradox and other Meditations on Management.* This discussion is based on the latter half of the article cited in the Harvey book, published in 1988 (see above citation).

[10] Palmer, P., *Healing the Heart of Democracy*, Jossey-Bass, San Francisco, 2012.

[11] This type of mature leadership is clearly hard work; that's why we included Appendix A as a "one-stop shop" for leadership and power references. Please refer to that resource for additional insights.

[12] Consider the 19<u>th</u> Amendment (Women's' Suffrage) which was finally ratified on August 18, 1920, and the 13<u>th</u>, 14<u>th</u> and 15<u>th</u> Amendments, which were only ratified after the Civil War concluded.

[13] https://www.pewsocialtrends.org/fact-sheet/the-data-on-women-leaders/

[14] We finally beat our own record for highest percentage of female CEOs of Fortune 500 companies from 6.8% in 2017 to 7.4% in 2020 - how thrilling. https://www.google.com/amp/s/fortune.com/2020/05/18/women-ceos-fortune-500-2020/amp/.

[15] https://www.airforcetimes.com/news/your-air-force/2019/11/13/gen-maryanne-millers-message-to-new-airmen-its-all-about-character/.

[16] https://womenintvfilm.sdsu.edu/wp-content/uploads/2018/09/2017-18_Boxed_In_Report.pdf. In fact, only five women directors have been nominated.

[17] https://www.statista.com/statistics/737923/us-population-by-gender/#:~:text=How%20many%20women%20are%20there,million%20men%20in%20the%20U.S.

[18] https://fortune.com/2020/05/18/women-ceos-fortune-500-2020/

[19] https://nwlc-ciw49tixgw5lbab.stackpathdns.com/wp-content/uploads/2018/10/The-Wage-Gap-Who-How-Why-and-What-to-Do-2019.pdf

[20] https://nwlc-ciw49tixgw5lbab.stackpathdns.com/wp-content/uploads/2019/03/AAPI-EPD-1.30.2020.pdf

[21] https://www.cnbc.com/2020/02/12/michelle-obama-on-famous-catchphrase-when-they-go-low-we-go-high.html

[22] Portions of this essay are based on a previous blog post by the au-

thor on <u>LinkedIn</u>, entitled "This Had to Happen - My Thoughts on the George Floyd Murder," June 4, 2020.

[23] Glaude Jr., E., *Begin Again*, Crown Books, Kindle Edition. (p. 24).

[24] Douglass, F., "If There Is No Struggle There Is No Progress"- From a speech also called "West India Emancipation, in Canandaigua, NY, August 3, 1857. https://www.blackpast.org/african-american-history/1857-frederick-douglass-if-there-no-struggle-there-no-progress/, accessed July 31, 2020.

[25] Glaude Jr., *op. cit.* (p. 27).

[26] *Ibid*, (p. 102).

[27] "The Arc of the Moral Universe is Long, But it Bends Toward Justice," from a speech given by Dr. Martin Luther King, March 31, 1968, who was inspired by the writings of the 19th century Unitarian abolitionist Theodore Parker.

[28] See: AZ Quotes, accessed, July 30, 2020.

[29] See: "Together, You Can Redeem the Soul of Our Nation," by John R. Lewis, July 30, 2020, accessed July 30, 2020.

[30] LinkedIn blog post. *Op. cit.*

[31] Barber, W., "America must listen to its wounds. They will tell us where to look for hope," The Guardian Online, May 30, 2020, accessed July 30, 2020.

[32] Fisher, M., "Read the most important speech Nelson Mandela ever gave," Washington Post, December 5, 2013, accessed July 30, 2020.

[33] Moore, J. "We Are Obligated to Exercise Our Humanity For Humanity." *HuffPost*, HuffPost, January 17,2017, www.huffpost.com/entry/we-are-obligated-to-exercise-our-humanity-for-humanity_b_587e9826e4b0b110fe11dbb9, accessed July 28, 2020.

[34] Lally, R. *Police Use of Fatal Force Identified as a Leading Cause of Death in Young Men*, <u>Rutgers Today</u>, University Research and Innovation, August 8, 2019, www.rutgers.edu/news/police-use-fatal-force-identified-leading-cause-death-young-men, accessed July 28, 2020.

[35] Shamsian, Jacob. "24 Things You May Have Missed in Childish Gambino's 'This Is America' Music Video," Insider, October 24, 2018, www.insider.com/this-is-america-music-video-meaning-references-childish-gambino-donald-glover-2018-5, accessed July 28, 2020.

[36] BlackPast. (1964) Malcolm X's Speech at the Founding Rally of the Organization of Afro-American Unity, BlackPast, September 23, 2019, www.blackpast.org/african-american-history/speeches-african-american-history/1964-malcolm-x-s-speech-founding-rally-organization-afro-american-unity/, accessed July 28, 2020.

[37] Johnson, A. "50 Years Later: Remembering Fred Hampton" Radioproject.org, "Making Contact," 3 Dec. 2019, www.radioproject.org/2019/12/50-years-later-remembering-fred-hampton/, accessed July 28, 2020.

[38] Carl Hunt and Joshua Hunt assisted in the writing and editing of this essay. Also, thanks to Dr. Brian Arthur for his inspiration from an earlier interview Carl Hunt did for a previous article.

[39] Arthur, B., "Complexity Economics: a different framework for economic thought," Santa Fe Institute monograph, March 12, 2013, accessed July 16, 2020.

[40] The 1918 pandemic is often referred to as the Spanish Flu, which is ironic because Spain was little affected. American politicians dubbed it that to deflect attention from the fact that it most likely arose at an Army base in Kansas.

[41] See also Arthur, *ibid*. Arthur weaves the concepts of emergence and complexity throughout this excellent paper.

[42] As late as 1939, lone academics (Burke, 1974) and writers (Orwell, 1968) were warning Western scholars and leaders to take Hitler and his *Mein Kampf* seriously as a battle plan. It was obviously too late. Hitler invaded Poland September 1, 1939.

[43] Interestingly, this is a bit of a paradox for people who have rejected the sciences that have predicted and helped us mitigate the virus and long-term economic damage, as it will be these same sciences that provide treatments and vaccines to help us overcome COVID-19.

[44] The greatest driver of homicide is inequality (Daly, 2016), although social scientists have no consensus as to why this is. The poor rarely if ever rise in revolution, instead elites who wish to challenge the status quo use inequality and popular grievances as a rallying cry to mobilize support (Brinton, 1964; Kuznar, 2007).

[45] It's worth noting there is only one "intelligent" crew that could bring about change: humanity. The other important thought is that

this crew rarely pulls together nor thinks of their ship as one unified crew might.

[46] Stuart Kauffman, MD, wrote the Foreword to this book. He has been studying complex systems such as the earth and its environment for 60 years. He was Carl's academic advisor and dissertation director from 1998-2001, and Carl has known and worked with Dr. Kauffman since 1997. The description of *The Adjacent Possible* and the *Theory of the Adjacent Possible* are used with the permission of the author of these concepts, Dr. Kauffman.

[47] Highlighted in Hunt C. and Kauffman, S., "Envisioning a post-crisis world," https://blog.oup.com/2020/05/envisioning-a-post-crisis-world/, Oxford University Press Blog, May 12, 2020.

[48] Buckminster Fuller Institute: "Spaceship Earth," https://www.bfi.org/about-fuller/big-ideas/spaceshipearth, accessed July 21, 2020.

[49] Friedman, T., "How We Broke the World," New York Times Op-Ed, May 30, 2020.

[50] UN Report: Nature's Dangerous Decline 'Unprecedented'; Species Extinction Rates 'Accelerating,' May 6, 2019, accessed July 7, 2020. This is also substantiated and updated in the World Wide Fund for Nature's Living Planet Report of 2020, accessed on September 10, 2020.

[51] See a formal definition for the Anthropocene at http://www.anthropocene.info/.

[52] Almost ten years ago, science writer Steven Johnson wrote *Where Good Ideas Come From: The Natural History of Innovation*, (Riverhead Books, 2011). An influential business and innovation history book, Johnson's work helped to popularize an idea that Kauffman introduced almost ten years earlier in his own book, *Investigations* (Oxford University Press, 2002).

[53] See also the more extensive discussion on *emergence* in Chapter 1, Power and Paradox, and Appendix B, Emergence and Complexity.

[54] See also Lawrence Kuznar's discussion of "Complexity Economics" based on the work of Dr. Brian Arthur, reviewed in Chapter 5, Power in the Post-Pandemic Economy. Arthur's work presents an excellent complement to the work we discuss here on the Theory of the Adjacent Possible.

[55] Kauffman and his colleagues, Wim Hordijk, Mike Steel and Roger Koppl proposed and refined the Theory of the Adjacent Possible "formula" throughout meetings and collaborations in 2017. Kauffman and his collaborators began proposing it formally in a variety of peer-reviewed papers, which Kauffman discusses in a video presentation posted on December 4, 2019. At this writing, Dr. Wim Hordijk is a "Wandering Scientist at Large," possibly hiking the Austrian Alps in the summer of 2020, Dr. Mike Steel is the Director of the Biomathematics Research Centre at the University of Canterbury, Christchurch, NZ, and Dr. Roger Koppl is a Finance Professor at the Whitman School of Management at Syracuse University.

[56] World GDP Growth, https://ourworldindata.org/grapher/world-gdp-over-the-last-two-millennia, accessed July 9, 2020. Original Source Data: Our World in Data, University of Oxford, Licensed under Creative Commons.

[57] Friedman, T., "Make America Immune Again," https://www.nytimes.com/2020/05/05/opinion/coronavirus-us-immunity.html, NY Times Op-Ed, May 5, 2020.

[58] In this current essay, we will not directly address the faults of the Framers and the new Constitution to deal with "America's Original Sin" of codifying slavery and maltreatment of Native Americans. It does appear from contemporary correspondences of the time and additional source documents that some hoped Article V could be used to ultimately correct those wrongs.

[59] As a reminder from Chapter 1, Power and Paradox, a **Paradox of Power** occurs when a person or organization exercises authority in a way that reduces the potential of the group as a whole. It diminishes or destroys the possibility for an effective power relationship between leader(s) and follower(s). While the actions of the leadership may seem sound and reasonable, these actions create a contradiction that harms the organization.

[60] In his paper, "The Defense No. 1, [1792-1795]," Alexander Hamilton wrote "Party-Spirit is an inseparable appendage of human nature. It grows naturally out of the rival passions of Men, and is therefore to be found in all Governments. But there is no political truth better established by experience nor more to be deprecated in itself, than that this

most dangerous spirit is apt to rage with greatest violence, in governments of the popular kind, and is at once their most common and their most fatal disease." The dangers of continuing along this path are great. Hamilton concluded "Hence the disorders, convulsions, and tumults, which have so often disturbed the repose, marred the happiness, and overturned the liberties of republics; enabling the leaders of the parties to become the Masters & oppressors of the People." Hamilton describes an early realization of **Paradoxes of Power**.

[61] We learned about the potential outcomes of interactions in previous essays and the discussions on emergence and complexity in Appendix B. Often these interactions form their own "bonds" that can be very difficult to cleave.

[62] For instance, compared to other countries the U.S. has a moderate homicide rate (about 5/100,000), compared to countries like South Africa (34/100,000), or the highest El Salvador (about 83/100,000). And this rate is much lower than what has been typical in human history; archaeologists have established that approximately 1/3 of all males died of homicide among our tribal ancestors (Keeley, 1996; Pinker, 2011).

[63] The following section was written by Carl Hunt. He was a registered Republican through the Reagan and George H. W. Bush years, even voting for Bush 41 for a second term. He then was Independent until the Obama election at which time he registered as a Democrat. While not a political scientist and hardly an expert, he's seen and thought about politics from a variety of perspectives, both domestic and foreign, following the exceptional curriculum of the National War College. Nonetheless, the views presented in this section are his own.

[64] Bacevich, A., *The Limits of Power*, Metropolitan Books, NY, 2008, (p. 10-11).

[65] See also Krugman, P., "The Cult of Selfishness Is Killing America" New York Times Op-Ed, July 27, 2020, accessed July 28, 2020.

[66] See for example, Perlstein, R. "Lee Atwater's Infamous 1981 Interview on the Southern Strategy, Nation Magazine Online, November 13, 2012, accessed July 28, 2020. Nixon did have the so-called Huston Plan that began to embrace a strategy that sought to significantly divide the country along several lines, including regionally. Fortunately for the nation, Nixon found resistance to executing this plan

against his fellow Americans due to protests from his Attorney General and from the leadership of the FBI and CIA. Under Reagan, Atwater and the Southern Strategy appears to have jumped into high gear.

[67] Think here about Hillary Clinton's "basket of deplorables."

[68] Political scientist John Campbell (2018) provides an incisive analysis of candidate Donald Trump's appeal to various population segments who were left behind by the nation's progressive elites.

[69] This discussion is led by Lawrence Kuznar, the essay team's resident academic.

[70] See Letter of Thomas Jefferson to Richard Price, January 8, 1789: "A sense of this necessity, and a submission to it, is to me a new and consolatory proof that *wherever the people are well informed they can be trusted with their own government*; that whenever things get so far wrong as to attract their notice, they may be relied on to set them to rights."

[71] In addition to Defense research, DARPA has been the sponsor of science and technology in the service of humanity such as space exploration (NASA), and was the originator of the Internet.

[72] Hattox, Ralph S. *Coffee and Coffeehouses: The Origins of a Social Beverage in the Medieval Near East*. (Wiley, 1985). It is interesting that the popularity of coffee over-rode these restrictions. It is further notable that coffee shops are standard features near universities to this day.

[73] We borrow the Declaration's convention regarding gender here, fully understanding that such a statement covers both women and men, regardless of race.

[74] Alinsky began writing on radical and violent confrontation in the 1940's (Alinsky, 1946).

[75] The story of the incident and her apology and eventual dismissal are well covered in this New York Time article by journalist Richard Pérez-Peña: https://www.nytimes.com/2016/02/26/us/university-of-missouri-fires-melissa-click-who-tried-to-block-journalist-at-protest.html.

[76] Nichols, T. *The Death of Expertise: The Campaign against Established Knowledge and Why it Matters* (Oxford University Press, 2017)

[77] Or in politics, for that matter.

[78] The quoted phrases are in reference to the hubris exhibited on the

left by presidential candidate Hillary Clinton made on September 9, 2016 "You know, to just be grossly generalistic, you could put half of Trump's supporters into what I call the **basket of deplorables**. Right? They're racist, sexist, homophobic, xenophobic – Islamophobic – you name it..." and on the right Senator Rick Santorum in a speech at the Values Voter Summit on September 15, 2012 "We will never have the media on our side, ever, in this country. **We will never have the elite, smart people on our side**, because they believe they should have the power to tell you what to do. So our colleges and universities, they're not going to be on our side."

[79] This is in reference to a meeting of extremist doctors who support right-wing causes and President Donald Trump. The President was particularly interested in the views of Dr. Stella Gwandiku-Ambe Immanuel on hydroxychloroquine and the futility of masks. In addition to her views on COVID-19, she blends her Christian beliefs with animistic beliefs in spiritual spouses and conspiracy theories about aliens to explain reproductive illness. After meeting with the President and having Facebook take down her posts as misinformation, she was granted audience with Vice President Mike Pence.

[80] We invoke David Hume in splitting this chapter out from the previous chapter, as we intended to make it one in the beginning. Chapter 7 reflects what is supposed to be objective: Government and Education (government strongly influenced, dare we say polluted, by politics); Chapter 8 reflects on those things that are inherently moral: Religion and Justice. Here we claim David Hume's "is - ought" distinction.

[81] Carl is the primary author of this section on religion and writes the following: "I feel it's important to disclose that I am what I consider to be a 'practicing Christian.' I could also characterize myself as a 'reformed evangelical' who has become more of a 'live and let live' mainstream protestant these days. While I no longer attend a local church, I feel my relationship with God through Jesus Christ is not only important but fundamental to who I am. I believe Grace makes such a relationship possible and in my individual case necessary. As it says in Ephesians 2, 8-9: 'For it is by grace you have been saved, through faith—and this is not from yourselves, it is the gift of God—not by works, so that no one can boast' (NIV). In any event, this relationship is between God and me,

and no one else."

[82] Article VI of the US Constitution: "no religious Test shall ever be required as a Qualification to any Office or public Trust under the United States," and the First Amendment to the US Constitution: "Congress shall make no law respecting an establishment of religion, or prohibiting the free exercise thereof;..." together being the only mentions of Religion in our founding documents.

[83] Conservative intellectual George Will, a self-proclaimed "amiable, low-voltage atheist," provides an insightful reality check on the importance of religion in U.S. history and contemporary society in his essay, "Religion and the American Republic," *National Affairs*, 44 (Summer 2020), https://www.nationalaffairs.com/publications/detail/religion-and-the-american-republic.

[84] The Quotes of President Dwight D. Eisenhower, "Address at the Freedoms Foundation, Waldorf-Astoria, New York City, New York, 12/22/52" Presidential Library, The National Archives, accessed August 5, 2020.

[85] Matthew 25:35: "For I was hungry, and you gave Me something to eat; I was thirsty, and you gave Me something to drink; I was a stranger, and you invited Me in." (New American Standard Bible)

[86] Matthew 23:23: "Woe to you, scribes and Pharisees, hypocrites! For you tithe mint and dill and cumin, and have neglected the weightier provisions of the law: justice and mercy and faithfulness; but these are the things you should have done without neglecting the others." (New American Standard Bible)

[87] Deuteronomy 10:19: "So show your love for the alien, for you were aliens in the land of Egypt." (New American Standard Bible).

[88] Sider, R., *The Spiritual Danger of Donald Trump: 30 Evangelical Christians on Justice, Truth, and Moral Integrity*, Cascade Books, Eugene, OR, 2020.

[89] 1 Thessalonians 5:21, New American Standard Bible Online, accessed August 12, 2020.

[90] Lawrence and Carl jointly wrote this section. Carl seeks to bring his personal experiences to bear as both a former Houston, Texas police officer and as a retired US Army Military Police officer on this deeply important issue.

[91] Smith, M., "Incremental Change Is a Moral Failure: Mere reform won't fix policing," https://www.theatlantic.com/magazine/archive/2020/09/police-reform-is-not-enough/614176/?utm_source=email-promo&utm_medium=cr&utm_campaign=kendi-cover-prospects-A, Atlantic Magazine, September, 2020 (Online Edition, accessed, August 8, 2020)

[92] See Chapter 1, "Power and Paradox," for a reminder of the potency of *being on the bus*.

[93] Carl provides the observations noted in the first and second subsections.

[94] Note the emphasis was on "excessive" force, not justified use of force. This country needs to have a debate on better defining these principles. How police use force has long been unchallenged.

[95] Mill., J., *On Liberty*, 1859, now available through Dover Publications, March 1, 2012.

[96] Jerrold Packard documents the rise of Jim Crow laws and their effects on the United States in his *American Nightmare: The History of Jim Crow* (SMP Publications, 2003).

[97] Dr. David A. Schum was Carl's academic advisor and dissertation co-director at George Mason University, and a genuinely great national intellectual resource who is sorely missed.

[98] This phrase is engraved above the main entrance to the United States Supreme Court in Washington, DC.

[99] Some of the essayists have commented on how our current levels of national political dysfunction began well before 2016, as specifically addressed in Chapter 7 by Lawrence Kuznar and Carl.

[100] We should also note that with proper resources, some of these questions might feed into a broader effort by a research firm or academic institution that might feed the great need for our nation to better understand itself and our emergent diversity.

[101] These topics are also discussed by Veronica Mata in "What Gives You Your Power?" dated August 17, 2020, and "Why We Wrote This Book, Part II," by Dennis W. Greene and Carl W. Hunt, dated August 24, 2020, both posted on the Paradoxes of Power website.

[102] In posing this question about a new "American Narrative" we rely on the definition of a narrative as being a cohesive story we tell about

ourselves to each other and to the rest of the world. In the case of a new narrative, we hope that it would be based on objective facts and experiences…as things are, not necessarily as we might like (wish) things to be. Of course, our aspirations to build a continually better narrative would include the latter.

[103] For comparison, there are currently 535 members of the US Congress (100 Senators and 435 Representatives). An additional 50 Senators would bring the total to 585 members of Congress, still well below the total of 650 Members of Parliament, in the UK, not including the House of Lords. While the two governing systems are not fully comparable, it does demonstrate the practicality of more national-level legislators, particularly given that the population of the UK is roughly 68 million people versus the population of the United States of about 331 million.

[104] For a more detailed discussion of this important consideration, see Wegman, J., "The Electoral College Will Destroy America," New York Times, September 8, 2020, accessed September 9, 2020.

[105] It's worth debating, and will be no doubt be debated in the 2020 elections, that "law and order" principles are both useful for maintaining a focus on peaceful protest, and at the same time, a so-called "dog-whistle" to both urban and suburban white communities to exacerbate fear of "invasion" of non-white residents who allegedly bring new forms of criminal activity and disruption with them. There are Democratic claims that the latter assertion has become a mantra for the current GOP-lead administration…undoubtedly this will be part of the debates between the two parties.

[106] Franklin D. Roosevelt's First Inaugural Speech, March 4, 1933.

[107] White, L., "Energy and the Evolution of Culture," American Anthropologist, (1943), 43, 335-356.

[108] https://www.eia.gov/tools/faqs/faq.php?id=87&t=1

[109] See Appendix B, Complexity and Emergence, for more detail on these concepts.

[110] Tracy, R., et. al., "Small Business Loans Helped the Well-Heeled and Connected, Too," The Wall Street Journal, July 6, 2020, https://www.wsj.com/articles/u-s-releases-names-of-biggest-ppp-borrowers-11594047600, accessed August 30, 2020. Verified through

PolitiFact (Poynter Institute).

[111] Dua, A., et. al., "COVID-19's effect on jobs at small businesses in the United States" A McKinsey & Company business report, May 5, 2020, https://www.mckinsey.com/industries/public-and-social-sector/our-insights/covid-19s-effect-on-jobs-at-small-businesses-in-the-united-states#, accessed August 24, 2020.

[112] See the Wikipedia pages on Alvin Toffler's books for a quick recap on his thinking. The three books referenced above were published in 1970, 1980 and 1990, respectively.

[113] Hunt, CW and Hunt, CE, "Renewing American Vigor: Transforming Consumption and Production," 2014, https://www.academia.edu/18866663/Renewing_American_Vigor_Transforming_Consumption_and_Production, accessed August 30, 2020.

[114] This is not a value judgment on Donald Trump's presidency. Historians use the same "era" term for previous administrations. Each era demonstrates power malfunctions, or **Paradoxes of Power**.

[115] Porter, W., and Mykleby, M., "A National Strategic Narrative," now maintained at the National Committee on American Foreign Policy, https://www.ncafp.org/national-strategic-narrative-vision-america-age-uncertainty/, accessed on August 27, 2020. A 20-minute video presentation of the Narrative is presented at: https://www.youtube.com/watch?v=q5aBOjhoiCw&t=1s.

[116] Ibid.

[117] Ibid.

[118] Javanbakht, A., and Saab, L., "What Happens in the Brain When We Feel Fear," Smithsonian Magazine (Online), October 27, 2017, accessed September 3, 2020.

[119] Carl W. Hunt, co-editor of this book, contributed to parts of this Appendix.

[120] Hersey, P., and Natemeyer, W., "Situational Leadership and Power," Classics of Organizational Behavior, Waveland Press, Long Grove IL, 2011.

[121] Hersey, P., & Blanchard, K.H., "Life cycle theory of leadership," Training & Development Journal, 23(5), 26–34. 1969. Further refined in Hersey, P. and Blanchard, K. H. Management of Organizational Behavior

– *Utilizing Human Resources*, Prentice Hall, New Jersey, 1969 and subsequent versions, and labeled as "Situational Leadership."

[122] Rogers, M., "Instrumental and Infra-Resources: The Bases of Power," *American Journal of Sociology* 79, 6 (1973): 1418–1433.

[123] Burns, J. M., *Op cit.*

[124] R. M. Stogdill, *Handbook of Leadership* (New York: Free Press, 1974).

[125] Hersey, P., Blanchard, K., Natemeyer, W., "Situational Leadership, Perception, and the Impact of Power," *Group and Organizational Studies* 4, no. 4 (December 1979): 418–428.

[126]Adapted from Hersey, P., *The Situational Leader* (Escondido, CA: Center for Leadership Studies, 1985), 27.

[127] Etzioni, A., *A Comparative Analysis of Complex Organizations* (New York: Free Press, 1961).

[128] Machiavelli, N., "Of Cruelty and Clemency, Whether It Is Better to Be Loved or Feared," *The Prince and the Discourses* (New York: Random House, 1950).

[129] Beene, K., *A Conception of Authority* (New York: Teachers College, Columbia University, 1943).

[130] French, J., and Raven, B., "The Bases of Social Power," in D. Cartright, ed., *Studies in Social Power* (Ann Arbor: University of Michigan, Institute for Social Research, 1959).

[131] Raven, B., and Kruglanski, W., "Conflict and Power," in P. G. Swingle, ed., *The Structure of Conflict* (New York: Academic Press, 1975), 177–219.

[132] Hersey, P., and Natemeyer, W., "The Changing Role of Performance Management," *Training and Development Journal* (April 1980).

[133] For the most recent textbook-based presentation on "Situational Leadership," see Hersey, P., Blanchard., K, et. al., *Management of Organizational Behavior*, 10th Edition, Pearson Education, Inc., Saddle River, NJ, 2013.

[134] Steven Kerr, "On the Folly of Rewarding A, While Hoping for B," *Academy of Management Journal* 18 (1975): 769–783. Reprinted with commentary in *The Academy of Management Executive* 9, no. 1 (February 1995): 7–14 and an informal survey, "More on the Folly," 15–16.

[135] Peters, T., "Power: Get It and Use It with These 13 Secrets," *Star Tribune,* August 2, 1994, 2D.

[136] Natemeyer, W. "An Empirical Investigation" collected for use by

North American Training and Development, Inc.

[137] *Ibid.*, Hersey, Blanchard, and Natemeyer, "Situational Leadership and Power."

[138] Burns, *Ibid.*

[139] *Op. Cit.*, From Burns section entitled "The Two Essentials of Power" in which he describes the interrelated nature of motive and resource, they come together to build relationships of power.

[140] *Op. cit.*

[141] This section is supplemented by the thoughts of Carl Hunt, the co-editor of this book.

[142] Hersey, P., and Natemeyer, W., "Situational Leadership and Power," *Ibid.*

[143] For a deeper explanation of these concepts in the context of leadership, see Hunt, C., and Natemeyer, W., "A Future for Leadership in Secure Cyberspace Operations," posted on academia.edu, https://www.academia.edu/30465796/A_Future_for_Leadership_in_Secure_Cyberspace_Operations, accessed August 3, 2020.

[144] Obolensky, N., *Complex Adaptive Leadership: Embracing Paradox and Uncertainty*, Ashgate Publishing Ltd., Kindle Edition, 2014, p. 55.

[145] *Op. Cit.*

[146] Wikipedia definition of the term paradox, https://en.wikipedia.org/wiki/Paradox, accessed July 9, 2020.

[147] Dwight D. Eisenhower, "Public Papers of the Presidents," 1959, taken from <u>Remarks at the National Defense Executive Reserve Conference</u>, 1957, published by the University of Michigan.